THE SEVEN WINDOWS TO WHOLENESS

BY

JAMES L. CRABTREE

Bloomington, IN Milton Keynes, UK

AuthorHouse™
1663 Liberty Drive, Suite 200
Bloomington, IN 47403
www.authorhouse.com
Phone: 1-800-839-8640

AuthorHouse™ UK Ltd.
500 Avebury Boulevard
Central Milton Keynes, MK9 2BE
www.authorhouse.co.uk
Phone: 08001974150

First published by AuthorHouse 6/21/2006

ISBN: 1-4259-4710-7 (sc)

613.0

Library of Congress Control Number: 2006905684

Printed in the United States of America
Bloomington, Indiana

This book is printed on acid-free paper.

TABLE OF CONTENTS

ACKNOWLEDGMENTS

I am most grateful for the support, assistance, editing, spiritual teaching, and general encouragement provided by my wife, Maril. Without her, it's hard to imagine this book even being in existence – and if it did exist, it wouldn't be nearly as good as it is.

I am also grateful to all of my clients and students over the last fifteen years of my practicing these difficult arts of healing and teaching. They have been my teachers, and it is their wisdom and experience shared with me that has led to the discoveries and material in this book. I become a little more knowledgeable and a little wiser every time I have an experience with a client or student.

The clients I quote or talk about in this book have been given different names and slightly different circumstances where necessary to preserve privacy.

PART ONE

DISCOVERING THE SEVEN WINDOWS TO WHOLENESS

CHAPTER 1

WHAT THIS BOOK OFFERS

"Who's the happiest person you know?" My friend Toby asked me the other day.

"Why are you asking?"

"It was a question at our group the other night, and we were thinking of all the possible people – the Dalai Lama, Bill Gates... like that. Who do you think of?"

"Me," I said.

As I spoke I realized that I am the most joyful, happy person I know. I feel good about my life and look forward to each day, each new event, each happening with a delighted and confident feeling of an abundant universe that will provide whatever my heart desires. I feel connected, full of purpose, and whole.

This doesn't mean I don't have "bad" days, anger, sadness, grief, upset, pain, disease, or any of the other things that used to "cause" me to not be joyful. But I have a larger perspective on my life and more

1

consciousness of my worth and lovability on a minute-to-minute basis. That consciousness keeps me in touch with the bigger picture of how things fit, and as a result I feel happy and fulfilled.

In the last several years, by an incredible series of unexpected events, the outer world has changed to match my inner experience. First I became expanded, whole and filled; then the universe cooperated by bringing me more and more expansion, wholeness and "filledness."

This didn't happen by chance. I discovered a process for allowing me to be connected to a complete sense of wellness. That process changed me.

That process can also change you.

This process – I call it "opening the seven windows to wholeness" – was given to me to share with others, which is the purpose of this book.

How It Can Work for You

What is missing in your life? Do you have physical conditions that interrupt your ability to feel happy, fulfilled, and satisfied? Do you have a feeling of something lacking? Are you stuck? Are you discontent? Do you even wonder why you're here on earth?

What is out there to help you? What have you tried? You may have tried to discipline yourself. You may have seen all the right professionals, read self-help books, medicated yourself with prescriptions, over-the-counter drugs, alcohol, or food – but nothing has alleviated the discomfort on a permanent basis.

There is a solution.

There is a bigger/wiser you who knows the solution, even if you haven't been able to connect with that "bigger/wiser" you.

This book offers a way to experience that connection in an ongoing, day-to-day way.

When you really know and *are* the bigger/wiser person that is already a part of you – then your experience of yourself changes.

You feel connected; you feel content and happy; you feel a sense of well-being – in short, you feel healed and "whole."

Let me give you an example. Marcy used the approach offered in this book and changed her life.

She says:

"The biggest change is in how I deal with problems, disappointments, and life in general. I now listen to what my inner voice/gut tells me. I have a lot more faith that what I need will be provided at the right time, when I'm ready to handle it. I am much more open to people, more thoughtful, compassionate, and more giving of myself. This whole process has been very rewarding to me as I was not really happy before this, and now I'm more content."

Or consider this succinct comment by Alice:

"I don't know if things are actually better or whether I'm reacting to them better." Either way, Alice has found a new way to approach her life.

Marcy and Alice both have discovered that they can be happy, content, and feel centered and connected without waiting for all of their pains to be cured, their issues to be resolved, or their life circumstances to become perfect.

Many of us believe we can be happy as soon as we fix what's wrong. We can be fulfilled/satisfied/okay "as soon as" we...

> quit having the pain, or
> have more money, or
> get a different partner, or
> lose thirty pounds, or
> quit smoking, or
> finish our education, or
> etc., etc., etc.

What if inside you there is a person who is able to transcend the irritation and distraction of those "things-that-are-wrong" and be really optimistically excited about you, your life, and what's going on with you – no matter what? This is not a Pollyanna attitude, but is an actual experience of what's really in your life from the perspective of the whole you.

This bigger/wiser you lives from a perspective that transcends the daily distractions of your life and allows you to understand and enjoy what life offers, and to leave behind struggling and suffering. You experience life as an effortless flow.

I know it's possible because I've done it.

How to Get There

As an energy healer, I first shared Opening the Seven Windows to Wholeness as a technique for promoting healing in my clients. Those clients' responses convinced me that this was good for them. Teaching other energy healers to bring these techniques to their clients has broadened the availability. However,

4

this process doesn't have to be performed by an outside healer.

Using this book, you can administer the techniques to yourself in seven steps.

The book describes and illustrates each of the seven steps, and assigns self-guided exercises – called Energy Tools – for absorbing each step into your energy field. You can use these tools for the actual work of transforming your energy body, and thus changing your life.

No two people will have exactly the same results from using these seven steps.

As you read through the experiences I have had, and the clients' experiences, you will start your own process of making this connection. Then, use the steps as they are written: the order – starting with the fable at the beginning of each step – is intentional and is a part of the process that will help you set aside your normal way of approaching and accomplishing transformation. The fables speak to a different part of your brain in each step, and the exercises reach beneath emotions and beliefs to move and change them through energy.

You can use the Energy Tools in a group as well as alone. When small groups commit to undertake these seven steps together, the individual efforts are reinforced. The book includes suggestions for how to conduct exercises as a group, how to reflect together on various aspects of the wholeness journey, and how to keep a "group journal" of insights as a result of the group's wholeness work together.

The group option will answer a need in some people for a community where they can be authentically known, and where they can receive ongoing support for their healing efforts. Others will find it exciting to take the journey "solo" by creating a space in their lives to do this work.

Once you have successfully completed these steps, you will experience and connect with yourself and your life in an unmistakable way. From that moment on, you will live from a different, and joyous, understanding of what your life is about.

CHAPTER 2

MY JOURNEY TO EXPANSION

Where I Started

I certainly didn't always feel this inner peace and contentment. I was a trial lawyer, with a wife and two kids, a house in the suburbs, and all the trappings of a successful life underway.

I felt the pressure to make enough money to support our lifestyle, and was something of a hypochondriac – being especially afraid of heart attacks or life-threatening diseases. All you had to do was tell me about an illness and I began to come down with it.

Louise was a legal client who had a bad heart and diabetes and was in a serious car wreck. About a year after the wreck, I traveled to her Arkansas town to prepare for depositions. I could see she was using a walker and not getting around very well, and asked her to describe her physical condition.

"My low back hurts all the time. When my back hurts, my legs hurt. Whenever the pain is worse in my back I get shortness of breath and pain in my chest – and I get scared that I'm having a heart attack. I also feel real shaky and have a 'sicky' feeling. And then I'm afraid I'll just pass out and die."

It was evening when I was there. I could see the obvious pain and strain she had.

I went back to my motel, went to bed, and woke up in the middle of the night with back pain, shortness of breath, a "sick" feeling, and a pain in my chest. I was very afraid, and the back pain was so bad that I filled the bathtub with hot water and tried to relieve the back pain first. I also knew myself well enough to know that all the pains, shortness of breath, and fear of death were probably just out of sympathy with my client.

The next morning I was miraculously well.

This hypochondria wasn't a good trait for a lawyer whose clients coped with a variety of serious personal injuries or diseases.

During this period of my life, I smoked too much, drank too much, and worked too many hours.

In spite of my professional and financial success, I had a lot of anxiety and experienced a lot of worrisome physical symptoms. Most of the time I was unaware of my emotions and feelings.

I realized that something needed to be done – I just didn't know what.

I changed jobs two or three times, hoping that a better work situation would make me happier.

It didn't work. I still spent too many hours glued to my job and spent too much time away from my family.

One highlight of my life was a weekly group that met to discuss social issues. I enjoyed the group very much. One day June, a member of the group, said, "Let's go out of town for a weekend retreat – leave Friday night and come back Sunday evening, and have an extended time together!" Everybody thought it was a good idea, but I had a problem.

"I have to work Saturdays, so we would need to leave later, or I'll have to miss part of the time." My friend Dustin argued with me.

"You can take off one week end."

"No, there is a really heavy trial docket coming up, and I'm lucky to get here for the one week night."

Dustin: "You can control how you spend your time."
Me: "No, you don't understand, I HAVE to work.
Dustin: "You never HAVE to work, you CHOOSE to work."

This really struck me. I didn't feel I had a choice – the consequences of not working were too grim to contemplate. I still felt victimized by those negative consequences: I didn't want to miss the group and I felt I couldn't give up my work. I was unable to find a good option.

That incident is an example of the way I was "locked in" by my perception of reality.

I believed there was more to reality than we were taught, and intellectually knew there were more choices, but I had no experience that supported that knowledge. I didn't know what to do to have more choice.

Still, I was progressing. I kept trying to understand more, study more, and do what I could. And I had done some things: I tried to work less, I stopped smoking, I considered not drinking alcohol any more.

But nothing was basically different. I was always working out of others' expectations, always trying to prove myself, and still felt I was missing something.

I had not always been missing it. Until I was thirteen years old, I had a very different perspective. An event at that age changed the course of my life.

When it Left

I had put off the exploration long enough! Tonight, I was determined to make the journey.

I went to my room, lay on my back, shut my eyes, and let myself drift.

For as long as I could remember, when I went to bed I played a game with my mind. I connected my consciousness – or whatever lay "inside" my head - to a tunnel. That tunnel went deep inside me, then seemed to open out and connect me with something beyond. I wasn't sure what it was – but I knew that when I needed information, I went to that tunnel.

Usually, I waited at the end of the tunnel and let the information come to me. Tonight, I gathered my conscious awareness along with my courage and started moving into the tunnel. I went deeper and deeper.

The tunnel opened onto a vertical cliff, and I moved to the very edge of the opening.

Before me glittered the entire universe. I was at once connected and separate: it was huge, revealing me to be a tiny speck. Though the universe was bigger than anything I could imagine, I had a feeling of belonging – as if everything and everyone was inviting me to join them. I felt an urge to jump off the cliff, or wherever I was, and let myself surrender into the hugeness. I also felt a strong urge to stay right where I was.

Then the thought occurred to me, "If you get lost, or can't get back, your folks will find an insane person lying on your bed."

Reason prevailed – but what actually prevailed was terror!

I felt totally overwhelmed with vertigo, fear of the unknown, and my smallness in the face of such grandeur.

I raced back out of the tunnel. I wanted to keep away from that place.

When people in my part of the country drilled for oil and found none, they would "dry-cap" the hole, filling the opening with cement – so that no animals or children could accidentally fall into it.

At the age of thirteen, I "dry-capped" that tunnel inside me. I visualized filling it with cement, then covering over the entrance so that I would never again be tempted to tumble into that place.

I had no idea that twenty years later, as I explored the exciting edges of new spiritual growth, I would do everything I could to find my way back to that tunnel. All it meant to me then was that I needed to limit myself as my culture taught me to. I needed to learn and to work within the systems and not allow my own independent connection with the universe to guide me. In short, I told myself that reality began and stopped where my culture said it did.

My Big Wake-Up Call

I was jolted out of my limited perception of reality at my sister's funeral. Just after she turned forty, Jackie was killed in a car wreck by a drunk driver, speeding head-on on the wrong side of the road. Death was vicious and instantaneous, and – as those kinds of deaths are – totally unexpected.

The weekend after her death was surreal. We immediately drove five hours to be with my parents. The night after the accident, my eighteen-year-old daughter, Virginia, couldn't sleep in the room where Jackie used to sleep. Virginia was awakened by a bad "more-than-a-dream" where her aunt apparently expressed frustration, anger, and confusion by trying to come back into her room. Frightened by what seemed to be an experience with a ghost, Virginia slept on a couch the rest of the night.

On the morning of the funeral, as I sat in the funeral parlor, Jackie seemed to come to me and express her wish that I look after our parents, since she had gone on. I felt that it was really she, but it was a quiet and subjective experience, and I discounted it as a part of the emotion surrounding her death..

After the funeral service, however, something happened that I couldn't dismiss, and wouldn't want to if I could.

My folks wanted to ride in their own car, so they had parked their brand new Chrysler New Yorker just behind the limousine. My wife, Maril, and I were going to take them to the gravesite. We came out of the funeral parlor with Mom on my arm, and Maril escorting my Dad just behind us. We were the first people out.

When we were about forty feet from the empty car, its horn started honking. The sound broke the silence of the morning, and continued for what seemed like forever!! (probably actually only about ten seconds).

Then it stopped.

The silence was as deafening as the noise had been.

We had picked up our pace – I wanted to get to the car and try to stop the horn – but it stopped just before we got there. I have no recollection of speaking, but my Mother heard me say, "Oh, Jackie!"

As we got in the car, Mom asked, "Do you think it was really Jackie? Did she honk the horn?"

"I'm sure it was," I said. "Maril, please write this down because we're not going to believe this really happened later unless we can read it."

My Dad, a Western Kansas skeptic, piped up from the back seat. "It must be a short; it's something wrong with the mechanism of the car."

"Well, I guess we'll know if it's a short if it happens again," said Mom.

I sat in the driver's seat, my hands resting on the steering wheel. "We'll never hear **that** again!" I replied.

Just then, the horn again honked, this time for one or two seconds and quit. As it honked, I saw and heard in my mind's eye Jackie giving the sort of laugh/

snort that always accompanied her moment of saying, "Gotcha!!"

After that incident, the horn only honked when someone pushed on it.

I was completely awed by the experience. There was no question that we had just experienced my sister from wherever she was.

That night my folks told me that since high school, whenever Jackie came back home to visit them, she always gave a resounding honk of her car horn as she pulled into the driveway. My folks would turn to each other and say, "Jackie's home."

I didn't immediately understand how important this event was in my life. I stopped drinking then. But I saw that as my reaction to Jackie's death from a drunk driver.

And I wanted to put the "horn incident" in the category of "weird things that can happen when someone dies."

On the other hand, this experience was personal; it made sense; my sister was the kind of person who would jump outside the bounds of societal restrictions in order to do what she thought was right ("What do you mean, I can't honk the horn to show them I'm ok? Watch me!). I had the choice either to pretend it didn't happen, or to let it make sense in my understanding of how the universe works.

Years before, I had read *The World Beyond* by Ruth Montgomery and *Seth Speaks* by Jane Roberts and had an intellectual idea that reality was bigger than I thought. As I researched further, the whole concept of an energy force as a part of our every-day reality seemed more and more likely.

Starting to Wake Up

I have already mentioned that I'm conservative about jumping into radical changes. It was two years later before I took any action, and then it was initiated by someone else.

"Hello, Jim, this is Doris," I heard over the phone. "Are you serious about this 'healing' thing?"

That was actually a good question to ask me. Doris is a nurse/teacher and I had mentioned to her how my studies had led me to believe more about an energy field surrounding our physical bodies. I had expressed the idea that I needed to pursue energy healing as a possible way of understanding and expanding what I knew. But, as usual, I hadn't really arrived at any specific action to take. Now, as I considered the question (guiltily), I said, "Yes, I guess so."

"Well, if you are serious, you need to come Thursday night to hear this woman at the Nursing College. Her name's Delores Krueger."

On Thursday I learned that Delores Krueger had founded "Therapeutic Touch" – a healing modality now taught in many nursing schools. She had done studies that showed an actual physical change in the charge of hemocrits in the blood from energy work. At last, an objective sign of an effect from the energy force I had read about!

As a result of that lecture, I became involved with Therapeutic Touch. Three women who taught nursing in Kansas City and I (the lawyer) formed a group to

15

practice and learn about it. This fairly mild form of healing can be very effective. Even though it's called "Therapeutic Touch," we actually worked with our hands two to three inches off the body in the energy field.

I made some astonishing discoveries in that therapeutic touch group. First of all, I actually experienced – and could control and change – what my energy was doing. This brought in a new element of reality. I didn't yet "see" the energy, but I felt it.

I also experienced how helpful and important my using that energy might be.

After we had been meeting weekly for almost a year, I received a phone call from Bonnie, a member of my faith community, who had had a serious car accident.

"Jim," she said, "I'm having a lot of trouble. I just got out of the hospital. I can't yet walk. I have one broken leg that goes up into the pelvis. You should see the bruises – still! – and it's been ten days since the accident."

"What happened in the wreck?" I asked. I thought she was calling because I was a lawyer, and she might be interested in bringing a lawsuit for personal injuries. As she described it, however, it was clear that there was no other driver involved in such a way as to support a claim. Instead, Bonnie had another request.

"You said last month that you've been doing Therapeutic Touch; I want to recover as fast as possible, and I'm doing everything I can. Of course, there will be physical therapy, but I'm also consulting a nutritionist, and I've been doing some visualizations. Could you possibly work on me with the Therapeutic Touch also?"

"I don't know how good at it I am yet," I said." Are you sure you don't want to ask one of the other more experienced people?"

"No." Bonnie was definite. "I feel like you are the right person." With some trepidation, I agreed to do a session at her home.

I went to Bonnie's place. She was lying on a couch, not yet able to walk. I still experienced some fear about whether I could be a benefit for her, but decided simply to do the techniques I had learned, and trust the work to do what it was supposed to do. ("Trust the work" has forever since been my mantra when faced with a situation where I have doubt or fear about the efficacy of energy healing.)

Therapeutic Touch involves holding the physical hands about three inches from the body and letting the necessary energy run through the healer to balance the energy field. I started in the area of her feet, working up the body, with particular time spent at the specific places where there was pain, and where the fractures were. As I finished, Bonnie said,

"That's amazing! The pain is so much less than it was. Thank you."

I was really pleased; this was a basic confirmation for both of us. We did weekly sessions for about six weeks until she was both on her feet and pain free.

Bonnie's recovery was much quicker than her doctors had predicted. She was walking, and then walking without a cane, weeks before they expected her to. They were surprised, but she and I knew that the energy work had been an important part of her self-healing.

You would think that that experience alone would cause me to jump immediately into a more active study of energy healing.

But I continued to experience the resistance to change. My excuse was my involvement with my profession, family, and community. I was really "too busy" to devote any more time to energy work.

CHAPTER 3

THE PREPARATION PERIOD

In early 1990 Maril and I flew to the Caribbean for a private a spiritual retreat. We spent some time doing exercises from a variety of meditation and energy books, talked about what the present and the future might hold, and spent one entire day in silence and listening.

One of the books we took along was *Hands of Light* by Barbara Brennan. I had owned this book for about two years, and had never read it.

The night before leaving for the Caribbean, Maril and I attended a philosophy lecture. As the presenter talked, I actually saw his energy body a little. It was a really funny shape, sort of bottle-necked with a wide bottom.

One evening on the island, Maril was lying on the bed, with *Hands of Light* open to a page that had several pictures of energy patterns on it. I noticed one picture in particular.

"There!" I pointed. "That's exactly the shape I was trying to describe for the guy's aura the other night." We looked at the explanation written under the picture. It described the aura of "a man lecturing on his favorite subject."

I felt elated. I connected with the book, and avidly read it cover to cover over the next day and a half. As Maril and I talked about what I had read in the book, she noticed my excitement.

"Have you thought of contacting Barbara Brennan to see if she does some workshops?" she asked.

"That's a good idea; when we get back to the States I'll try to find her phone number. I'm also going to see if I can go to one of those week-long intensives on Therapeutic Touch."

I came back home, contacted the Therapeutic Touch teachers and found out that the two intensives I could go to were on the only two weeks I had previous commitments that precluded my going. However, I discovered that Barbara Brennan was conducting a four-day workshop in an available week. I attended that workshop. As I was packing the night before the workshop, I talked with Maril.

"I'm really nervous – I'm going to spend four days half a continent from home, I don't know anybody there, and I'm not even sure if this energy stuff is real."

"Right!"

"Oh, I know I've seen something (or think I have) a couple of times, and I've read all the stuff – I believe in it – I just don't know if it's something that I can do."

20

She smiled. "But isn't this a good place to find out?"

"Yes, you're right. I feel like one of three things is going to happen:

1. I'll get there and find out they're all a bunch of loonies, and this is just 'airy-fairy' stuff.

2. I'll get there, find out they are really doing and seeing something; find out it's wonderful; and it's so far beyond me that I can't even learn it; or

3. I'll feel like I've come home."

I didn't tell Maril, then, because I was afraid of looking too foolish – but deep inside me I already knew that I would have that "coming-home" feeling. I had recognized it when I first picked up the book.

The next day, as I walked up to the registration desk, I wasn't so sure. The workshop was held in a beautiful old Town Hall in Bridgehampton, New York. The area was unfamiliar to me, and looked like something out of a fairy tale illustration. The first person I saw wore a long flowing purple dress, was barefoot, and fit all my stereotype-fears of "new age."

The people at the registration desk, however, were down-to-earth. I met several other participants registering for the workshop who were "just like me." I started to relax into the excitement of the event.

Over the course of the next four days, my life was transformed. As we progressed from simple introductory exercises to more and more sophisticated ones, I discovered that I could perceive energy more than I could before, and that I had an expanded ability to experience and control my own energy, such as the amount of energy that I ran through my body, the direction it ran, how it connected to the earth, etc.

I also discovered that the system at that school was effective in teaching others; it was not just a showcase for our very talented leader.

At one point the speaker on the stage was talking to one of the participants, describing her energy system. Two recent graduates of the school, serving as teaching assistants in the workshop, were seated behind the speaker. As she continued, the teacher said, "I see that you are blocking energy in your solar plexus," and she gave additional information as to what that meant. As she talked on, I saw the assistant teachers looking at the participant, nudging each other, and whispering with concerned expressions. Just then, the teacher (who couldn't see the assistants behind her) said,

"Oh, no. I'm misreading that. The solar plexus energy is really open." As she went on to explain what that meant, the two assistant teachers breathed sighs of relief and relaxed back into their chairs. Obviously, they had seen the energy themselves, and seen that the misinterpretation was happening.

That incident confirmed for me that this wasn't a school that simply watched the teacher, without empowering the students.

When I came home from the workshop I brought with me the application to enter the upcoming fall class. I told myself, "You can't really go to this school – it is a huge time and money investment." A deeper part of me said, "This is something you are supposed to do." My internal voice continued to offer objections:

"You may never be able to do it well enough."

"Nobody you know can do any of this; you'll be totally alone."

"You'll have to cut back on the hours you put into your law practice; you already need to spend more time there."

"It means traveling to New York a week at a time, six times a year – being away from family and friends."

"You'll have to choose between law and healing."

I didn't dispute the "reasonableness" of any of those ideas. Nor did I feel particularly able to justify my sense of why I was to do this. It really went back to the kinds of feelings I got as a child when I sat in front of that tunnel and realized I needed to do something.

It's easy to make it sound like a hard decision. I was giving up a lot of comfort and couldn't see whether the benefit would be worth it. But in truth the decision was easy. I had such a deep sense of knowing that I was supposed to go. Not to have gone would have felt like giving up on myself.

I sent the application and prepared for school.

The School Years

I spent the next six years traveling from Kansas City to Long Island, six times a year for five or six days at a time, to study and learn there. The first four years I was enrolled in school and graduated in 1994; then I spent two years going back to the sessions as a teaching assistant.

23

These were years of great learning and discovery: how to perceive energy; how to see it; how to modulate my own energy field; what techniques to use for sprained ankle, cancer, depression, relationship difficulties, low energy, "I'm stuck in my life," and all the other myriad problems and illnesses people present to an energy healer. One experience stands out as a gift from the universe in solidifying what I was learning.

One day in my first year, we were learning how to hold ourselves at various levels of the auric energy field. At different energy frequency levels, the energy body consists of different properties, different colors, and is capable of different types of effects. Students have to learn to hold themselves intentionally at particular levels and to know where they are. My experience was that I could "intend" to be at the levels, do the physical things that we were taught to do, but I couldn't always tell what level I was actually on.

Our teacher had told us to hold the fourth level of the field, and that is what I was trying to do. She came over to me and stood there observing.

"What level are you on?"

"Four????"

I didn't exactly overwhelm her with confidence in the accuracy of my answer.

"Do you experience how precise everything is, how clearly you are thinking? "

"I do feel that."

"And what level of the field has those qualities?"

I knew that the third level was where that was true, and told her so.

"Good!" She said. "You are experiencing the third level, and now have a way of verifying that you are there. Now, put your hands in the area of the fourth chakra, let the vibration of that chakra come into your hands, and let that vibration spread through your whole body."

Following her guidance, I placed my hands at the level of my heart, the area of the fourth chakra or energy center.

"What is different now from when you were on the third level?" she asked.

I realized that there was a different sensation. The energy seemed faster, and there was an expanded feeling that I could identify – almost as if there were an energy umbrella forming a cloud above, around, and behind me.

My teacher said, "I can see that you are on the fourth level; remember and use this sensing to confirm it for yourself."

Now when I see students get to the point of developing enough perceptive experience to distinguish the levels of the auric energy field, I always recall how important that moment was. Until then, I could intend to be on a level, but had no personal experiential basis for confirming it. After that, I did.

Teachers who were able to see and confirm our energy experiences made the learning process infinitely easier.

A second gift from the universe came later in my training. I often was unsure of being able to do new skills when we were first told about them. By this time we were working in the astral field, and we were learning to remove what our teachers called "critters" (energy blocks with consciousness) from the energy field. When we were first taught this skill, I doubted that I'd be able to do it.

Students were working on each other; on this day, I was being the healer. We worked on massage tables; more than fifty tables stood in rows, in a large hotel ballroom. We were working in groups of two; one student was the healer and one was the client, with the client lying on the table, and the healer standing to one side. Our assignment was to complete an energy balancing, then go to where we perceived a "critter" in the client's field, and take it out.

I had done the balancing and was at the point of finding a critter. My client had mentioned that she had some discomfort in the stomach area, so I was scanning with my energy hand and looking for a critter there. To my surprise, I saw a little box-shaped thing that was black and had reddish-orange little circles on it (kind of like a reverse-colored lady bug); it also had a head and two antennae at one end.

Following the technique as taught, I reached in with my energy hand, took the critter, and lifted it out of the client's field. When I had raised my physical hand to about my eye level, I stopped. It was a very curious sensation – as I looked at my hand on the energy level, I saw the critter on it; yet when I looked on the purely physical level, my hand looked empty. Being able to see it both ways at once puzzled me.

As I was standing there, one of the teaching assistants came down our row and saw me holding out my hand. She said, "Oh, you have one of those black things with red spots, don't you?"

Those are just two examples of how my time at the school consisted of learning new perceptions and techniques, trying them out, having teachers and fellow students who could confirm the experiences, and finally incorporating them as my own.

I also learned that as I could move more energy through my body, my own understandings deepened, my own issues were revealed in deeper ways, and I continually had to go further in clearing myself as my energy sophistication increased. In addition to learning techniques, and expanding our high sense perception of energy, we spent time processing the fuller awareness of ourselves that was generated.

This inner work, while less glamorous than learning about energy, proved to be some of the most valuable part of the training – preparing me to be partnered with and to mirror my client in a helpful and present way, no matter what issues arose for them.

Both the inner work and the ability to perceive what I saw energetically signaled a transition of my own – from someone who wanted to learn about energy healing, to someone who had acquired the necessary knowledge and skill to offer my services in facilitating others in their healing.

As the years at school finished, I could see what incredible progress I made with understanding the Human Energy Field. In that time I reduced my involvement in the law, to the point that at the end of 1995 I turned my law practice over to my son, and I opened a "healing space" in an office building in a Kansas City suburb.

Cara

I had been in Naples visiting relatives, and a Kansas City friend had asked me to visit with the owner of a particular bookstore. The owner wasn't there, so I left my card. About an hour later, a woman named Tessa came in to the bookstore. She had been familiar with energy work in California, knew the Barbara Brennan book, and asked the person at the bookstore if there were any Brennan-trained practitioners in Naples. She was told, "No, but there was a man from Kansas City here awhile ago who is." Tessa called me the next day (after I had returned to Kansas City).

"My four-year-old daughter, Cara, has T-Cell Leukemia, and she is undergoing an extremely powerful and hurtful two-year protocol of chemotherapy. She gets very sick after the treatments, has terrible leg aches, and requires blood transfusions. Could you work with her, and when are you coming back to Naples?"

"I'm not really scheduled to come back right now,' I said, "but when is Cara's next chemotherapy session?"

"It will be in April, about six weeks from now."

I heard myself say, "I'll come back to Naples for it."

Because of Cara's size and age, I felt that three 20 to 30 minute sessions during the week would be better than blasting her with a huge amount of energy all at once.

Cara was a delightful child – quite precocious and a spiritually advanced being. She had a lot of courage and an irrepressible spirit, and in spite of all the assault her body was undergoing, we had a lot of fun during the sessions – plus Cara was free from leg pains, felt better and stronger, and did not need blood transfusions because her platelet count recovered so quickly.

Cara's parents were thrilled, and wanted me to return regularly when Cara had chemotherapy. Over the next two years, they talked to a lot of people, who talked to other people, and I ended up having a part-time practice in Naples.

Cara continued to do well, she finished the chemotherapy protocol, and the signs of leukemia vanished.

Between traveling to Florida, traveling to New York, and spending part time on my law practice, I did not have time to do any teaching or workshops. Part of my motivation for going to the New York school was to bring information and opportunity about the Human Energy Field back to the Midwest. I quit teaching in New York, wrapped up my law practice, and began to offer workshops, seminars, and classes.

More Learnings from Clients

By the end of 1998, I had done almost 3,000 individual sessions, and had increased my understandings and competence in the energy balancing and healing work. I had added "seeing" energy to the other high sense perceptions, and was in awe of the results and importance of the healing work.

Bernie

One of my clients was a forty-five-year-old owner of a small business who had been diagnosed with lung cancer. The doctors advised Bernie that it was inoperable and told him that he had six months to a year and a half to live.

Bernie pursued an aggressive path of self healing, involving nutrition, herbs, visualizations, and energy work. We did a series of ten sessions over a nine-month period of time. Due to all his efforts (and in part to the energy work we were doing), the lung cancer just disappeared. The doctors called it a spontaneous remission, but I saw how hard Bernie worked in order to bring this about. I also saw further confirmation that energy healing can have a profound effect.

Grace

I was also learning that the results were not limited to relief from physical conditions. One of my most profound lessons came when working with Grace.

Grace was a twenty-six-year-old pretty brunette with neck and back complaints, as well as chronic difficult sinus issues. She was also very depressed, constantly crying, and not able to function. Old friends dropped by and Grace was unable to greet them. She stayed in her room and cried the whole time they were there.

In her first session, I did a gentle healing and balancing, which was primarily aimed at creating a safe enough environment for her to do the work she needed to do. I was setting the stage for future sessions.

Immediately after the session, Grace noticed that she didn't feel like crying, that her sinuses had cleared up, and that she felt more relaxed and secure than she had for a long time. When she called to set up a second session, she reported that she had been able to go to work, and was feeling much better.

Grace's recovery and healing continued over the next couple of years. As she became safer, she was able to release more of her history and problems from the past, and her physical and emotional symptoms improved dramatically.

What I learned at that first session, however, was that I need never underestimate the ability of people to heal themselves – without waiting for the processes that I might think are important. Although I had seen the first session as "preliminary," it provided a profound experience of self healing in Grace. I saw how powerful energy balancing can be in affecting mood, depression, outlook, and all of the mental and emotional aspects of well-being.

Chelsea

I also learned how well energy work can respond in some areas that involve both the physical and the emotional.

Chelsea was a thirty-seven-year-old friend who had severe PMS symptoms. She experienced a lot of emotional difficulty in the days before her period, along with physical cramping and pain; her periods were very hard.

"Does that stuff you learned in New York have any effect on this?" she asked.

I replied (as I always did), "I don't know; let's try it and find out."

She had a session shortly before her period was to start. We did another session a month later; we skipped a month and did a third session the next month.

Her PMS cleared up completely: there was no more pain, very little emotional or mood swings, and the periods were much more comfortable. She was so excited that she referred her sister. Her sister experienced similar results and so have many women since.

Other clients showed up with a variety of conditions that included physical diseases, relationship problems, depression and emotional upsets, lack of energy, a feeling of energy being blocked, physical injuries, feeling lost or stuck spiritually ("there's no purpose to my life"), and other conditions or problems that signaled to them that something was wrong and needed attention.

Vivian

I also was given an example of how much our conscious mind can avoid seeing what is obvious.

Vivian, a thirty-six-year-old mother of four, came in complaining of feeling ineffective and powerless. This was especially the case in her relationships. Her ex-husband encouraged their daughter to say and do things that Vivian didn't approve of – but he had custody of their daughter, and Vivian could do nothing about it. The same sense of ineffectiveness showed up in her current marriage and in her friendships.

As we worked, I energetically cleared the relationship cords to her children, her ex, her husband, and her friends. But there was another cord that presented itself as being blocked. From guidance, I received the information that the cord connected her to a living male, and his name was "Vince" or "Vincent."

I asked Vivian who she knew named Vince or Vincent. She said she had a deceased grandfather named Joseph Vincent. I told her of the block and said that it didn't seem like him.

"Well, I have an uncle, who is a priest. They call him Father Vincent." I asked about her relationship to him, and she said it was good. He was also somewhat older than Vivian, and this cord relationship I was seeing seemed more contemporary. I asked her about any other "Vincents" with whom she might have a relationship.

She said, "No. The only other Vincent I know is my brother. But I never got along with him, and I haven't spoken to him in years."

Vivian is a smart woman, but she didn't realize she needed to reconcile or attend to her relationship with her estranged brother. This is a good example of how we often don't see the obvious when it is about ourselves.

Morris

I also received some lessons about what "healing" is. Probably the most dramatic example was Morris.

Morris was a sixty-four-year-old man who was a healer in a neighboring town. He came to see me two months after a heart attack, complaining of shortness of breath, loss of appetite, and high pulse rate. He was medium height, with white, thinning hair. His smile had an elfin quality and his gentle eyes twinkled. As he talked about his condition, however, I felt the energy of terror, and saw a huge block in his upper chest – above the level of his heart.

I asked him what he was here for – and he talked about healing "this bad ticker." When I worked with him, however, what came up was how afraid he was, and I talked with him about that fear. He then said that what he really wanted was to be okay with whatever happened. As a healer, he didn't really believe that death was the end, but his emotions weren't matching his intellectual belief. The more we talked, the more he moved into that place of terror.

We did two sessions, which included removing the large block from his chest, after which he reported that the shortness of breath was somewhat better. He had also come to an acceptance of whatever the future might hold, including death. I observed that the energy obstruction in his upper chest and throat (where he had been holding that panic) was gone.

Three months after the session, Morris died in his sleep.

A friend of Morris's expressed the regret that my healing efforts hadn't worked for Morris – since he'd died anyway. I didn't say anything. But I realized that Morris had received exactly what he needed from our work together. The "healing" was to let go of the fear; it was not about "curing" his heart condition.

This was an important confirmation for me. I had intellectually grasped that concept while I was in training at the School, but to see it in action, and to understand the true nature of healing helped prepare me for the next step.

I Had Come So Far; and Had So Far to Go

At the end of 1998, things were going well for me. I worked hard doing individual sessions. My clients experienced a lot of healing. I started expanding my teaching and developed a three-year program for those who wanted to study healing. I was more in touch with my feelings, and had improved and broadened my awareness of unconditional love for myself.

I was still, however, operating from the secret knowledge that I was flawed. I was forty pounds overweight and had a variety of physical ills that I ignored, denied, and covered up because they were inconsistent with my image as a healer. I faulted myself for not having the self-discipline to do something about all of these things. I was still too busy, still working out of others' expectations, and always trying to prove myself. 1 knew I was missing something. I was doing what I wanted to do, but there was a quality of coercion involved – almost as if I were forced to live up to my own and others' expectations. I still longed for inner peace, and for something that I could not name.

CHAPTER 4

THE SEVEN WINDOWS

In 1999 I continued a daily practice of concluding my morning meditations with a time of seeking guidance through "automatic writing." I sat at the computer, with a pre-typed question or simply a sentence typed stating that I was willing to hear what I next needed to hear. I allowed my consciousness to move as if it were floating out of my body and let the energy of my guides come through and take control of my fingers. I trusted the process. I had received a lot of valuable information about the nature of the universe and about specific clients who were coming to see me on a given day.

On February 24, 1999, the following guidance came through:

> *"The Joy of Healing. A primer on how to make yourself whole. A primer on how to realize your wholeness and have fun doing it.*

Face it. Every self-help book out there tells you how to do a lot of things that are good for you; a lot of things that will help you heal; a lot of things that will change your life for the better: but they all make it sound like you're going to have to really "knuckle down" and discipline yourself; and it won't work if you don't go day to day getting better, trying harder, working more.

Well, that is all ok. And you can do that if you want to: and in fact it is necessary to do all that in a hard way – sacrificing stuff, and walking the 'narrow path' – if that's what you believe you have to do.

What is true is this:

1. *You are ALREADY whole.*

   The wholeness of you lies buried in a covering of blankets that keep you from realizing it: these blankets are called different things, but they come from belief system distortions, and resulting feelings that cloud you.

2. *You are unaware of your whole-ness because of your belief system distortions.*

3. *Within you the knowledge already exists as to how to clear up the distortions.*

4. *Aligning with the intention to recognize your wholeness is the first step.*

5. *You don't have to change to be whole.*

6. *Awareness of your wholeness will change you.*

7. *Being aware of your wholeness is more fun than living in ignorance of it.*"

The guidance went on to say that people could use the energy body to make these changes, and that techniques for working with the energy body corresponded with the seven "windows" to wholeness that were listed. The specific techniques for accomplishing the steps were not, however, included in the meditation.

I realized that something special had come through that morning, and immediately began to contemplate how to apply the wisdom I'd received. I also realized that I didn't know the energy techniques to get to this wholeness. I put the writing aside, and continued in my practice and teaching.

In looking back, I also realize that, much like Vivian in the example above, I missed the obvious: I thought of the guidance as offering me a way to work with other people – and gave no thought to the possibility that it might also be aimed at me.

Bringing the Seven Windows Home to Myself

As I continued with my healing practice and teaching, I also continued my pattern of resistance to personal change.

After graduating from the healing school, I expanded my knowledge by reading and studying books by teachers, healers, energy workers, and others in related fields. Annually, I had also taken a trip to experience another healer or teacher – often from a quite different modality – so that I could broaden my own understandings, improve my healership and teaching, and not get caught in the illusion that I already knew it all.

I heard of a healer in Brazil who was quite different from me, doing some remarkable things. He saw 200 or 300 people a day. People came from all over Brazil and other parts of the world to see him, and he was reportedly doing some "visible" surgeries – actually cutting on people with non-sterilized instruments, without anesthesia, doing rough stitching with one big needle, and having incredible healing results.

Only a small percentage of the people he worked on, however, had these "visible" surgeries. The rest were worked on by "entities" or guides that came to a room (the "operating room") in which clients were gathered to be healed as they sat in meditation ("invisible" surgeries). After some period of time spent sitting in the room, usually twenty to thirty minutes, one of the helpers in the room would tap the client on the shoulder, tell him/her the operation was completed, and she/he would quietly leave the room. Some of the clients sensitive to energy experienced these entities and their work; others did not feel anything during the session, but either way, many came away with dramatic healing experiences.

The healer worked as an "unconscious channel." Certain energies or entities (some of whom were deceased doctors in Brazil who still wanted to help heal people) came through him, while he was in a trance, and he remembered nothing of what happened while the healings were taking place.

I decided to spend a week in Brazil. I was not led to go for the reason of receiving healing (at least consciously), and I was not interested in doing what he does. But I was aware that things were happening for my clients every day in my healing room that would have seemed like miracles and were completely outside my experiential reality as little as ten years before, when I was practicing law.

Now, I understood that Joao de Deus (the Brazilian healer) was operating outside of my new experiential reality, and I wanted to be there and be able to understand if his type of healing would broaden my reality again, or if it would simply be that he was so far "out there" that I couldn't relate.

I joined a group led by a woman who had been to Joao's healing center several times before. About fifteen of us traveled to Brasilia by air and took car transportation to Abadania, a small village in Central Brazil. After we checked into a *posada* (a motel-like structure for accommodations, but with the added quality of serving boarding-house style meals), we assembled as a group, and our leader explained how Joao functions.

"He is down the road from here in a complex they've built. It is called *Casa de Dom Ignatio*, and Joao understands his work to be God's work. He uses the Lord's Prayer as his vehicle for going into trance. When we go there in the morning, there will first be a gathering of the people who have come for healing. They hold sessions at 9:00 AM and 2:00 PM each of the three days he is working this week. There may be several hundred people." We had already seen a busload of Brazilians who had ridden twenty-six hours to be there, so we were starting to get used to the numbers.

Our leader continued. "First, you'll hear a general presentation to the whole assemblage, which is done mostly by others, but Joao comes out and talks (in trance) for a part of it, and he will do any "visible" surgeries for the morning at that gathering. That lasts around an hour, then Joao goes back to the "current" room (a room where he and others sit in meditation and hold energy for the entities). The people then line up and each person goes in front of Joao, while he's in trance, and tells him what is needed or desired for healing. He'll "prescribe" what kind of operation is needed."

"He'll write on a slip of paper when your operation will be. That paper will have the time for you to come to the operating room to sit for your healing. Since it all happens in Portuguese, you'll need to work through a translator. They have one there, but tonight I'll have you tell me what you are here for, and I'll write it on a slip of paper that you'll give the translator when you are in front of Joao. He'll tell you anything Joao says in addition to giving you a piece of paper with your operation time on it."

I went there without a specific concept of what I wanted healed; but she asked us to name what we wanted. I knew that if I was to receive a benefit it would have to come from "outside the box" of what I could already name from the context of my mind, so I simply asked for "whatever the entities see as advisable."

The next morning, I joined the people at the *Casa*; we first saw Joao at the general presentation, heard the presentation (although since it was all in Portuguese, I didn't comprehend much of it), and formed a line to go before Joao. This line grows to a length of several hundred people, goes through the two rooms back to the room where Joao is seated, and extends back out the general area and down the street. When we got to Joao, we handed our notes to the translator, he told Joao, and Joao wrote the time of the operation and any further actions we should take (herbs, etc.).

Unlike most of the other people in my group, I was not assigned an operation the first time I went before Joao: he had me sit in the "current" – which is to say, sit in the room where people were filing before him, and help hold positive energy for them. This was not too unusual, for there normally are thirty to fifty people sitting in the room.

I went back through the process in the afternoon session. To my surprise, I was again told to sit in the current room – again not receiving assignment to an operation. I believed that maybe I would not receive an "operation" – perhaps because I didn't have anything specific in mind for healing

When I went back the next morning, however, I did receive instructions for an operation, but a very unusual one: instead of coming at 2:00 PM for the normal starting time at the operating room, I was told to come at 1:30 PM and lie on one of the four cots in the healing room. These cots seemed to be reserved for people that were very seriously ill, so I was somewhat perplexed by the assignment.

Promptly at 1:30 PM I presented myself as instructed. I was nervous, but the assistant told me to lie on the cot, and I did. For the first several minutes nothing happened – I lay there, trying to relax, feeling both scared and curious at the same time.

What followed was the most specific, dramatic, and profound healing experience of my life. Although it would have looked like I was just lying on this cot with a sheet over me, and no one around, I had a strong experience of three beings who were such a bright white light that it seemed as if they were parallel florescent lights coming from just above my head. They talked to me, invited some dialogue, and I could feel them working on different parts of my physical body. Instead of the twenty-minute time of most sessions, my session lasted until 4:00 PM. Although two and a half hours had passed, I couldn't tell if it had been twenty minutes or all day.

I knew that physical symptoms (in my knee and abdomen) were gone, and I had a strong feeling of something being different, but I wasn't aware of what healing had taken place. Most of my writings from the day or so after the session focus on the turn my life was taking, "re-wiring," and receiving a new spiritual guide. Later I came to understand that I had just been walked through the Opening of the first four Windows to Wholeness. Four of the seven steps that had been given to me one and a half years before were finally implemented in my own body.

Over the next six months, I was able to experience and go through windows five, six, and seven, so that the connection to the Wholeness Intention was finally brought into my own awareness.

During that same six months, I was given the techniques for helping others experience the process. I say "was given" because for all of my ego's desire to ascribe these techniques to some brilliance of my own, the wisdom came to me from the universe, from students, from clients, from servers in restaurants, from books and newspaper articles – literally from all around me. I have been a giant accumulator and receptacle for the wisdom of the universe. Now I was finally in a position to pass this wisdom on.

The Difference in Me

In the months immediately following my completion of opening the seven windows to wholeness, I easily lost the forty extra pounds I had been carrying around (it felt less like disciplining my diet and exercise and more like doing and eating what I really wanted). Most of my niggling physical symptoms just disappeared – acid reflux, right knee pain, a chronic cough I had had since having pneumonia in 1989 – and my exercise and running became easy and regular. I was probably in the best physical shape I had been for fifteen years.

But more profoundly, my experience of day-to-day life changed. I felt connected to and aware of a bigger perspective, so that I was always experiencing beauty and joyfulness of my life. I also became tolerant of the emotions, "defects," and other things that my personality did in reaction to life. Instead of judging myself, I knew that I was a beautiful person, connected to a greater life energy, and that the anger, pettiness, and various emotions were just reactions I had. These reactions became pieces of information and not evidence of my "badness" or "defectiveness."

This may not sound big – but as it hit me, it was huge! I relaxed into my own desires and goals, and gave up living for others (and my own expectations).

I also removed the words "have to" and "need to" from my vocabulary. I realized that everything was a matter of choice. Different choices carried different consequences, but nothing was really "forced" or "necessary." This also has made my life easier.

Most of the differences in my living were things that I had struggled to do for a long time. Now, however, I was not "doing" them; they simply were.

Probably the clearest way of describing it is that I was aware of two different levels of reality at once. I could observe the bigger picture, the beauty, and the connection as I lived; at the same time, my personality lived moment to moment with the same kinds of reactions I've always had. But when I responded in anger to a perceived slight (somebody cutting me off on the freeway), before I took it to action, the bigger/wiser me brought a more universal perspective. "Oh, look, Jim is still taking that personally, when he knows it isn't personal. That's what he does." And the observation was not judgmental, but interested, and looking for the underlying information that was being relayed. I freed up vast amounts of energy.

And then came the really unexpected surprise. As I settled into this new way of being, amazing events started happening. Maril and I had talked about wanting to go back to Hawaii, but were waiting for a little better financial picture.

Out of nowhere, I got a call from Emma, a friend and former client.

"I am going to be in a marathon in Hawaii, and I thought it was on Maui. Through my time share program, I booked a condo for a week on Maui. Then I found out the marathon is on the big island. So I have booked a condo there. However, I'm on the hook for the one in Maui, and can't use it. I thought of you – do you think you and Maril would like to take it? Oh, your cost would just be to reimburse me for what I had to pay – $250 for the week. Let me know if you'd like to take it."

I knew that $250 was more like what those condos cost for a night rather than for a whole week. Was I interested? You bet I was! But could we work it out?

Now I understand how synchronicity works with the wholeness so much more than I did: of course,

1) the week she was offering was a week when we had no other commitments scheduled (a rarity in our schedules);

2) I found a special on the airline fare that was less than half of what we had paid the last time we went;

3) our friend in Hawaii who runs a bed-and-breakfast knew a rental car dealer that gave us an incredible rate and so an entire ten-day Hawaii vacation appeared in our lives at a fraction of its usual cost.

That's just an example of the way things work now. Since connecting with the wholeness, times and places for retreats have appeared just when I needed them; amazingly profound sharings and learnings have been provided by clients, by friends, by whomever I meet. The information I need to hear is arranged for; all I have to do is pay attention.

My life is different in another way. I understand that my wholeness, my joyfulness, doesn't depend on any of these life circumstances. I'll be happy and joyful as my way of being in the wholeness – or I won't. And the circumstances don't dictate that.

I let go of the illusion that I'd be happier when circumstances were better. Then the circumstances actually got better.

If circumstances continue to be wonderful, I'll be grateful and joyful. As things occur that aren't "wonderful," I'll be grateful and joyful. If circumstances become "horrible," my choice is to remain grateful and joyful. I can do that because I continue to stand in the bigger place where "circumstances" are temporary and fleeting, and not the real or whole picture.

A quick confession: sometimes I've spent as much as a couple of days in a funk of forgetting, but I've come out of it much faster, and with better perspective, than when I used to spend weeks, months, or even years mired in that place. I suspect I'll continue to get better and better at keeping the wholeness perspective as I continue to live my life.

Clients' Experiences of the 7 Windows

As I brought the seven-step process to clients, it became apparent that this is meaningful and valuable for others also.

When the first fifty people had gone through the seven windows, most had noticed some powerful change – particularly in how they experience life. The over-all effect is readily apparent from Jill's experience:

"I changed dramatically because of the seven windows. Friends, family, and even acquaintances noticed a difference in me. I felt like I went from being a lonely, confused, sixteen-year-old girl to the confident, independent, twenty-five-year-old woman that I am. Several of my health ailments were less bothersome. The fibromyalgia wasn't as debilitating, the side effects from my medicine weren't as life-interrupting, my periods were not severe PMS, I had less anxiety (socially and situational), the mood swings were less frequent. I no longer was an addictive personality. I developed a relationship with a man unlike any I had in the past – it is an easy, enjoyable friendship and partnership. I learned a lot about myself during the process and continue to learn.

I often pause to wonder who I would be today if the seven windows to wholeness had never entered my life."

CHAPTER 5

EVOLUTION OF THE HEALER

While working as an energy practitioner with clients from all walks of life and with an enormous variety of needs, I went through several phases that eventually led me to the discovery of the Seven Windows to Wholeness. Ultimately, I have found that the key to experiencing wholeness is to change one's own self at the deepest, or most foundational, level, and to connect with what I now understand to be "the Wholeness Intention." Here's how I discovered that:

1. When I started, I expected the energy techniques to work on clients as drugs or medical procedures work on patients. The same technique applied to the same condition should produce the same result. But it didn't.

2. Next, I explored the possibility that the effectiveness of energy work depended upon the client's own readiness to accept the energy techniques. Maybe the effectiveness had to do with the client – not the technique. This focus improved the results somewhat, but didn't explain what was going on, and still portrayed my limited understanding of the nature of humans.

3. As that understanding of the nature of humans increased, I stopped perceiving "Intention" as just another element of the energy field, and came to realize that Intention is a deeper and different part of humans. I saw that Intention is beyond the energy field, has different properties, and operates differently from energy. I was then able to identify that place of Intention that knows all of us to be whole.

This last discovery was critical to my understanding. We "believe" we are whole; however, we operate as if we are flawed. It's as if our "knowing" that we're flawed trumps our "belief" in our wholeness. In that deeper, different part of humans – the Intention Realm – our true intent of wholeness exists. Aligning with that Wholeness Intention allows us to transform our experience.

The Wholeness Intention, however, carries a very different framework from how we are in this culture. Opening the Seven Windows to that Wholeness is a process that allows us to accomplish the radical shift from "flawed" to "whole."

Energy Healing: Different Results for Different

Clients

1. The first major phase of discovering the nature of healing came from my frustration because of the different results my clients experienced for the same problems. Why did different people receive such different results from the same work? Some people reported great changes from the energy work, while others noticed no lasting effects. Here are three examples:

Ann came in for her regular appointment, working on being balanced, centered, and having more energy. She arrived with the obvious symptoms of a cold.

"I want you to work on my allergic reaction to the new loft apartment Al and I moved into. The moment we moved in I started having an allergic reaction," she said. "I'm having a hard time breathing, lots of congestion, coughing, and sneezing. A good night's sleep is impossible."

I asked, "Is it possible you just have a cold?"

"No, because I get relief from the symptoms when I'm away from the loft for awhile."

I did a standard energy balancing, worked on her sinuses, and helped her align with an intention in the energy body that she be allergy-free.

The next day I got a phone call.

"Jim, this is Ann. It's wonderful! All my symptoms are gone.!"

"You mean, you didn't have the allergic reaction last night?"

"I mean exactly that!! I'm amazed – and so pleased!"

Her symptoms had disappeared. And they never returned.

A couple of months later, Lou came to see me with similar allergic reactions. I treated him with the same techniques. Unlike Ann, however, he experienced no improvement in symptoms.

Betty is a forty-one-year-old woman who had been coming to see me for awhile. On this day she seemed a little nervous.

"Jim, I would like to work on my low libido. My husband and I enjoyed sex in earlier years, but it has increasingly become a chore. I don't get much feeling, and so I don't have much enthusiasm for it. My marriage is suffering and we are growing apart."

I proposed a series of four treatments and worked with balancing the hormonal system. I also had her do a series of written exercises that would self-reveal where energy blocks might be held, and we then worked on releasing those blocks.

At her last session, she came in full of wonder. "Wow! Yesterday Rex and I spent 'intimate' time together, and I couldn't believe it. When we started I felt anticipation like I haven't felt in years. I stayed involved and excited through the whole thing."

Betty has continued to enjoy a good sex life with her husband.

I thought I'd found the keys to the kingdom! Sure enough, I soon had another client (call her Chris) with a complaint of low libido. We did the same type of series; same type of work; same hopeful cooperation from the client, but with no discernible result.

Bernie came to see me with a diagnosis of inoperable lung cancer. We did ten energy sessions over ten months, and he had a "spontaneous remission." His tumor went away and stayed away. He and I were both thrilled with the results. The next lung cancer client I worked with, however, showed no noticeable results in reducing or eliminating the cancerous tumor.

What caused these differences? I knew it had nothing to do with the amount of desire. Each of these clients sincerely "wanted" to heal.

Different Results Explained by Intention to Heal

2. For years, I thought the answer lay in the connection to the "intention to heal." I perceive a light in the energy body that connects with a client's intention to heal; when that light is blocked, the distortion seems to prevent the desired healing results. My most dramatic evidence came while I was still a student.

Eve came in as a new client. "I've done energy work before, and know a lot about it," she said. "Right now I'm really blocked energetically. My biggest problem is chronic low back pain, and that's how my energy block manifests."

I assessed her energy field, and noted that the "intention to heal" part of her energy was disconnected from its source, and that there was additional blocked energy in the back.

After finishing the hands-on treatment part of the energy session, I left Eve to lie quietly on the table for a few minutes, then returned with water, ready to give her feedback about the session. Usually clients lie there relaxing and absorbing the effect of the session. Eve, however, was sitting up and putting on her shoes.

She said, "Well, it didn't work. My back still hurts as much as it did."

"I'm really sorry," I replied. I noticed she seemed a little agitated, and that her focus was on the physical result. "Sometimes the physical relief comes a couple of hours after the session; perhaps you'd like me to talk about that and give you some feedback on what we did and what your energy body told me about you."

She said, "Nope! I've got to go!" She put on her shoes, and exited rapidly. I did notice that the energy connection to her intention to heal had remained closed.

My first conclusion was that I couldn't work successfully with a person who was disconnected from their intention to heal.

Later, I found that to be untrue. I can work successfully, but *first*, the connection has to be re-established with the healing intention. Only then can the substantive issue – be it back pain, emotional dysfunction, or cancer – be successfully dealt with.

If Eve were to come in with the same condition during this second phase of my understanding, I would have spent the majority of the first session on the *reconnection* of that intention to heal. Only then would I be able to work successfully with the back pain.

A More Complete Understanding

3. I continued to explore the area of "connection with healing intention" and to grow in my understanding of how healing takes place. Eventually, I realized that my conclusions were a little over-simplified. I had not recognized how different "intention" was from the psychological principle that I had considered it to be.

CHAPTER 6

THE ARCHITECTURE OF HUMAN BEINGS

Our healing is greatly influenced by the energy body at the level beyond the three-dimensional world we normally call "reality."

Humans exist in several simultaneous different states of being, which I refer to here as "realms." In addition to the material realm, there are the energy, intention, and core star realms.

We're all aware of the material realm of our existence: our physical body, our emotions, our feelings, and our belief systems. They are the knowable parts of ourselves that the majority culture in this Western civilization understands to be the "total human being."

This realm is where and how we experience our day-to-day lives. As you read this book, your mind grapples with the concepts, you feel happy, or bored, or upset, your physical eyes translate the words into images that your brain translates into concepts, you can feel your body coming into contact with the chair (or bed). All of these things are going on at the material level.

In addition, lots of events are occurring at the material level that you may not hold in your awareness: your heart is beating, you are breathing, you are reaching out to turn a page, or to straighten an uncomfortable article of clothing. Part of your brain is paying attention to your environment – noting if there are any unexpected changes that might put you in danger. The material realm is clearly a huge part of who we are as humans.

The Rest of the Picture

The other realms – energy, intention, and core star – each have different characteristics and qualities, which allow them to be a part of the overall human without conflicting. They interact with each other to allow us to function as humans. You can think of them as different dimensions. The bridge that gives us access to all of them is the energy realm.

Although they are different dimensions, the realms exist in the same space within and around the physical or material body. As an illustration, imagine water, or H2O.

- below 32 degrees, H2O is ice and has solid physical boundaries that hold themselves.

- At a higher temperature, the properties change – it is still solid (as water), but the boundaries are defined by the container;

- at an even higher temperature, it becomes steam: not solid and no fixed boundaries.

Yet, it is always H2O. Its chemical composition remains the same, even though its form changes.

We are like that. The realms overlap and exist in the same space. Unlike H2O, however, the different realms of human existence all are present at the same time. We perceive them by shifting our focus, not by changing the temperature.

The energy realm exists from the center of your physical body, extending beyond the body. This realm contains "blueprints" and reflections of:

- all of your physical organs, characteristics, and events that occur.

- all of your feelings and emotions,

- all of your beliefs, and mental processes.

- your underlying intention realm, and

- your core star realm.

A Single Point of Light: the Core Star Realm

The core star realm is the part of you that is connected to everyone and everything else. It existed before you were thought of as an individual, and will go on forever. Think of it as a point of light that connects with all the other points of light of the universe. You can find the energetic reflection of it deep in the body, between the solar plexus and the navel. This core star is clearly connected, but does not have a "personal" feel to it – it is universal.

From the core star realm, the next state of being is the intention realm. From this realm comes the decision to individuate (but not separate) from the universal light of the core star. When you individuate you come into the personality that is uniquely "you" in this lifetime. Individuation creates an illusion of separation from the center light of the core star. As I'll discuss later, the *illusion* that it is a separation lies at the base of many of our difficulties with wholeness.

The Prime Mover: the Intention Realm

The underlying intention realm forms and holds the template or framework for the energy body. The intention realm carries the seeds for the energy body, which in turn carries the seeds for the material realm. Intention precedes energy; energy precedes manifestation into the material or physical. You can think of intention as the architect; the energy body as the blueprint; and the resulting "building" as the human being walking around in three-dimensional time and space.

Another way to understand this important principle is to look at how we come to this life. When we decide to come into this plane, we form an intention to be this person. From this intention, then, the energy body forms. The energy body creates the specific methods and modes of accomplishing what is intended, forming our physical characteristics, feelings, and belief systems at the material realm. These physical, emotional, and mental states are where the intention gets "fleshed" out in material form.

To illustrate, imagine that Jane's life purpose (part of the intention) in a particular life is to enhance her experience of compassion. The energy body then forms to create open heart energy, but also to interrupt and block the energy with respect to self esteem.

This very block creates the motivation for compassion.

It works like this: at the material realm, Jane believes herself unworthy, but subconsciously hides and tries to combat that perceived lack of self worth by taking care of others. As she lives her life, she learns to value herself by affirming the work she is doing for others. As a result she has more compassion for herself. Valuing herself increases her capacity to experience compassion

This higher self value at the material realm is a direct result of her effort to compensate for her perception of unworthiness (as a result of the energy block).

How We Experience Healing

Sometimes, however, the living out of an experience on the material realm creates such discomfort ("dis-ease") or inability to change that we understand ourselves to be outside the boundaries of how we were intended to be. In other words, we understand ourselves to be in need of "healing."

We may first seek healing on the material realm, going to a doctor for physical symptoms, a psychologist or therapist for emotional symptoms, a teacher or wise associate for belief system difficulties.

Many times, however, the underlying energy body holds the experience in such a way that it is more difficult to make the desired changes/healing/learning at the material realm. People may then go to energy healers so that direct work with the energy body can provide a way to allow a new level of healing to be created at the material realm.

In the above example, Jane may have great difficulty making the changes necessary to bring her feelings and belief systems into a place where she has more self esteem. Working directly on the energy body to change the way it is holding, moving, and blocking energy accomplishes changes she might not have accomplished otherwise.

Energy healing, then, becomes a short-cut – a way to "tweak" the framework the *material* body is held in, so that different changes can happen in the mental, emotional or physical body.

Removing blocks from Jane's energy body relating to self-esteem, and integrating that energy with her heart energy, may allow her to set aside her belief of her unworthiness, and recognize herself to be just as worthy of loving and caring as the "others" she has been serving.

Sometimes, however, it is not the material realm, but the *energy body itself* that is being held in a framework that prevents the necessary change. That framework is the underlying realm of intention.

And so we return to the question previously posed: why can some people change with energy work, and not others?

A New Understanding of "Reality"

Many times, the answer to why some people change with energy work, while others see no discernible results, is because the underlying intention for the energy body is distorted.

Stop and look at that sentence.

"Intention," in this system, is different from the usual use of the term. It is an entire realm forming a part of us as humans, and is more powerful and subtle than if it were just a psychological principle.

While the energy body controls the material realm, intention controls the energy realm. When the energy body itself is held in distortion by the intention realm, *intention* must be changed to accomplish healing.

The Line of Intention

Changing the line of intention is like changing the foundation of a building – not to be undertaken lightly, and not an easy thing to do. Simply "wanting" to do it won't accomplish it. Even "intending" the change isn't enough, because there is a strong resistance to change. Changing the underlying line of intention means changing not just what we believe. It means, in effect, changing what we already *know.*

The line of intention – that all-important, invisible, hard-to-grasp part of ourselves that created our reason for being – forms our understanding of reality, what we *"know"* to be the way things work for us and for the world.

The full explanation for why some clients did not experience results from energy work, lies in the framework of their intention realm. In our examples, Ann's and Betty's lines of intention allowed for those changes in the energy and material realms; Lou's and Chris's simply didn't.

PART TWO

OPENING THE SEVEN WINDOWS TO WHOLENESS

I look around and see people suffering instead of rejoicing; working and struggling in an isolated way instead of flowing in a feeling of connectedness; dreading what might happen instead of eagerly anticipating; feeling unhappy, anxious, or depressed instead of knowing themselves to be happy; being in reaction to their life, instead of feeling in charge, responsive, and under control.

"Flowing in a feeling of connectedness," "eagerly anticipating the future with curiosity," "knowing oneself to be happy," and "feeling in charge, responsive and under control" are the results of what I call the "Wholeness Intention." To live from the center of the Wholeness Intention is our birthright; yet how to connect with it is omitted from our majority culture consciousness.

You can experience this connection or transformation for yourself.

You are not just going to learn to think or feel differently. The secret lies in learning how to use your **energy body** to connect in a different way to Intention. Then, the context for all of your experiences becomes drastically different. You live out your life differently – physically, emotionally, mentally, and spiritually – and you live in conscious connection with that Wholeness Intention.

We often are taught that "healing" ourselves must involve a lot of difficulty, pain, anguish, and is a long and tortuous process – and it can be. But it can also be a smooth and positive experience. My goal is to help you overcome the necessity for *suffering* and help you claim your natural state by a progression of exercises (energy tools) that help you prepare and change your energy body. The final exercise (the intention tool) helps you change the underlying Intention for your life.

CHAPTER 7

THE FIRST WINDOW: YOU ARE ALREADY WHOLE

You are already whole. Our culture does not teach this crucial information. Instead, the message is that if and when we add this quality, drop that quality, cure this disease, get more sleep, understand more, try harder, *then* we'll be "whole." *Then,* we'll be able to experience our power, our joy, our eager anticipation for each new day.

Overcoming that misperception is the first step in connecting with the wholeness intention. I hear some of you saying, "Well, I already believe that." And I agree. Believing this is something many of us do. The problem is that we forget it.

Ask yourself, "Do I live as if I believe it?"

- Do you have a genuine appreciation and respect for yourself that holds you in esteem as a wise and gentle being?

69

- Does the voice you talk to yourself with speak in the way you would speak to a revered teacher?

- Do you experience your wholeness as a complete, fulfilling aspect to your living of your life?

- Are you healed?

If you answered anything other than a resounding "yes" to any of these questions, you can increase your experience of wholeness.

The Story: Terri the '56 Thunderbird

Once upon a time in a faraway place there was a village where all the people were pretty much like the people where we live now. In this village lived a nice man named Doug who was in charge of collecting and displaying items of great beauty and worth.

One large garage in his collection contained a sample of each of the cars that he deemed beautiful and worthwhile. This garage had the cars lined up on display – there were Model A Fords and Model T's, Cadillacs and Duesenbergs, old models, and newer ones too. He had them arranged by year of manufacture, and he loved to walk up and down the rows of cars, looking at all of them. Other people of the village also came and admired the display.

Some days, he would go out into the garage and tinker with the cars – maybe fixing the motor on an old Studebaker, or re-painting a green Chrysler – just doing whatever improvements or repairs he felt like. Other days, he would take one of the working cars and go out for a spin – showing it off to the people in the village by driving it around.

Most of the time, though, he simply appreciated the cars.

There was one problem. Doug had never been able to find a 1956 Thunderbird. The display held an empty space for a 1956 Thunderbird.

We now turn our attention to another little village just around the other side of the mountain. In this village, again people were pretty much like where we live now, but additionally the automobiles were like people: they could talk, think, and even drive themselves.

The first car we see is Terri, who is a – guess what? – 1956 Thunderbird. Terri is sitting in her carport, at rest, with a full tank of gas. She is in good condition – no dents or scrapes – pretty red paint outside, and sparkly hubcaps. She looks like she's been driven a fair amount, yet is in pretty good shape.

But there is a huge problem. Terri doesn't believe she's a 1956 Thunderbird. She thinks she's a clunker – a post-wrecked 1956 Ford of indeterminate model. Her manual says she's a Thunderbird – and she'd like to believe it – but she knows too much. First of all, she has a bad spark plug that causes her motor to miss when she's accelerating. A Thunderbird would be able to get to 60 mph in 6 seconds – not cough around and take twice as long. Second, there are a bunch of mars and scratches in her windshield and headlights – so neither she nor her driver can see as clearly as they would be able to in a 1956 Thunderbird. Third, she doesn't *feel* beautiful – that absolutely proves she's not a Thunderbird, for Thunderbirds are beautiful and must know it. Finally, she's depressed and feels stuck. She doesn't know where she's going or why. If she were really a Thunderbird, she'd be clear and happy.

One fine spring day, an ad appears in the local paper in Terri's village: "Notice, 1956 Thunderbird needed for assuming its rightful place in collection of amazing vehicles!" Terri's friend brings the ad over, and suggests that Terri apply.

Terri, naturally, can't imagine applying. She's not qualified. Her friend tries to tell her she is, but Terri points out that she can't get from 0 to 60 in 6 seconds, she can't see clearly, she doesn't feel beautiful, and she's neither clear nor happy. Obviously she can't be a 1956 Thunderbird.

The friend notifies Doug, however, and Doug comes over to the village to inspect her. Lo and Behold! He finds just the car that will finish the collection. He has Terri moved over to his village and puts her into the spot that he has been saving for a 1956 Thunderbird.

Instead of feeling happy and thrilled to be chosen, Terri just feels like she doesn't belong. Somehow Doug has become terribly confused and has made a mistake.

When Doug finds out, he speaks with her: She says, "Obviously, I'm not a 1956 Thunderbird. I can't accelerate. The Thunderbird you're looking for would be able to."

Doug, however, says, "You are here because you are who you are – a Thunderbird. We can replace the spark plug so you can accelerate, or not replace it. But that won't change who you are."

"But Doug," says Terri, "I can't even see clearly. Maybe if you replace the windshield and head lights with unmarked ones, I can achieve the status of being the Thunderbird you want." Doug replies, "You don't need to change an accessory here and there, or even an engine part, to be a 1956 Thunderbird and fill this space I've held for you. Perhaps if we change the windshield and headlights so you can see clearly it will give you better function – but it won't change who you are."

Then Terri gets to the real meat of the matter: she neither feels beautiful, nor is she clear or happy. Obviously, she can't be the car of Doug's dreams until she fixes these deficits. Doug points out that Terri is creating the story that "feeling beautiful," "being happy," or "knowing where she's going in life," are matters that would change or affect who she is. Instead of letting any of those perceived mechanical or subjective defects define her ("I can't be a Thunderbird until I have fixed those"), she would be better served by recognizing her true nature — Thunderbird. Then she can be a Thunderbird who has a bad spark plug, instead of waiting until the spark plug is changed to recognize that she is a Thunderbird.

Terri doesn't really respond to Doug's invitation to perceive herself differently. She doesn't, that is, until one day...

Doug drives Terri out on a little sortie into the village, and he parks her right in front of a gigantic glass display window. Inside the window, Terri sees a beautiful, red 1956 Thunderbird.

"That's who I'd like to be!"

As she sits there, she suddenly realizes she is seeing a reflection: the car sitting there is in fact Terri herself. For the first time, she knows – really deeply "KNOWS" – that she is a 1956 Thunderbird.

Accepting this knowledge doesn't fix everything for Terri – she still has the spark plug and windshield that aren't perfect, she still doesn't know exactly where she's going, and she still gets depressed some days. She even still experiences feelings of being ugly from time to time. But her life has changed. She now accepts that those defects are just part of the over-all make up of "Terri, the '56 Thunderbird." And overall, even with those "defects," she is bringing to Doug and the village exactly what she was designed to bring:

She is the 1956 Thunderbird – she fills that slot.

She understands now what a gift that is. She understands that that gift does not depend upon her rate of acceleration, her emotional state, her opinion of herself, or whether her physical parts function perfectly.

Moral: You – who create beauty in the universe by your very being – can understand for yourself: "I am already whole."

The Bigger Perspective

How can you be aware of your wholeness? Your energy body contains all the powerful intention of your purpose for life, your connection to all of life, your experiences, and all of your qualities, characteristics, and aspects – both those that are already here and those potential ones that haven't yet shown up in material reality.

If you can learn to identify and experience all of yourself, including the energy body and all it contains, the question of your already having everything necessary for your life – already being whole – is answered.

Consider the following illustration:

A woman is looking out the window into the back yard. You can imagine her with smile on her face, and a twinkle in her eye. As she looks into the back yard she sees her two children playing. They constructed roads in a dirt pile and are racing cars.

"The red car is the fastest," Tommy says.

Josh keeps playing even though Tommy's red car wins two races.

Then suddenly Josh pushes the blue car forward faster. Tommy keeps moving the red car forward. At the finish line, they are very close. Each thinks his car won.

"The red car wins again!!!"

"No, the blue car won!!"

"Red car!!!"

"Blue car!!"

Josh is getting upset, his voice is rising, and it is very important to him that the blue car won. It's important to Tommy that his car, the red car, won.

Their mother is happy. It's a sunny day; her children are happy and healthy; they are playing in the fresh air of the back yard; they are even playing a game that may help them develop social skills.

Their mother could care less whether the red car or the blue car won.

This story illustrates our status. The mother in our story is the "wiser, bigger" you – you at the level of the energy realm, the intention and core star realms.

Your personality, your consciousness at the material realm, is the little boy, struggling with and contending for the winning of the issue that is before him: he wants the blue car (or red car) to win. At that moment the issue is so important that it seems to determine whether or not he can be happy in his life.

We spend most of our lives in the more-or-less forgetting position of those children – we invest huge amounts of energy and emotion in the "red car/blue car" issues. In fact, almost everything we contend for, that we get upset about, and that we struggle with is a red car/blue car issue. When we can stand back and see things from that bigger perspective, we see the true purpose and context for those issues, and our living experience completely changes.

As I will explain later, one of the most attractive aspects of the connection to wholeness is that it keeps the concept of healing in a positive context and doesn't make healing yourself the equivalent of a "negative" (that is, having a bad condition and removing it as the only way to be healed).

The Energy Tool below is the final step in implementing the first part of your own connection to wholeness – taking your own journey to a more joyful, fulfilling and satisfying life. You have incorporated the experience of the fable, others' experiences, and the underlying theory. These elements have prepared your energy body for moving to change. The Energy Tool shows you how you do it.

Give yourself all the time and attention needed to accomplish the directions in this tool. Find a time when you can be alone, uninterrupted, and have enough energy that you can fully attend to the task at hand. Have fun with it!

Energy Tool: Opening the First Window

This is a powerful self-healing method for you to open the first window in your material belief system and increase the experience of wholeness in your life.

1. Get some blank paper, a set of crayons, and a pen or pencil. Find a quiet place. If you like, put on some reflective music – preferably something without lyrics.

2. Spend a few minutes paying attention to your breathing, quieting your mind, and letting yourself relax. Focus on listening to the nothingness of the most-quiet place in your mind.

3. Accept and set as an assumption for this exercise that your energy body is whole, complete, and filled with all the elements that could provide for your experience of wholeness.

4. Allow your mind to visualize the vibrant patterns of colorful energy that make up your energy body. Remember, you are not focusing on any of the blocks, or any of the "stuck" places where wholeness is lacking – you are assuming that your energy

body contains everything it needs to be healthy and whole (this is true, whether you experience it at this point or not). Sit for several minutes in that reflection.

5. While maintaining silence, and without particularly thinking it through, pick up the crayons and draw your energy body as you visualize it in wholeness. Do not worry about the quality of the drawing; simply allow yourself to select colors based on what feels whole, and let the shape or shapes be whatever seems appropriate, with no censoring of your mind, eye, or hand as they connect this vision.

6. When you have finished the drawing, set it aside. Shut your eyes, relax and be still, and let your thoughts simply go where they want.

7. After a few minutes, put the picture of your energy body in front of you and look at it.

8. Take another piece of paper and list the elements or qualities of wholeness reflected in the drawing you have done. List them by looking at the drawing and see what it suggests to you. (You might, for example, see a part that suggests peacefulness, or intelligence, or compassion.) Again, you are focusing on the elements of wholeness; you will have a chance in later exercises to identify anything that isn't whole or doesn't feel like it is part of the wholeness.

9. Close with whatever reflections you have about the exercise. Express appreciation to the total being that is you for being willing to do this process.

10. Keep your wholeness drawing and your list in a place where you can refer back to them in future exercises.

Thank you for your participation.

CHAPTER 8

THE SECOND WINDOW: YOU ARE UNAWARE OF YOUR WHOLENESS BECAUSE OF YOUR BELIEF SYSTEM DISTORTIONS

You have just seen how you possess everything you need for whatever you intend in your life. Why wouldn't you automatically know, understand, and accept that fact as you live your life?

Your wholeness lies buried in a covering of "blankets" that keep you from realizing it: these blankets are called different things, but they come from belief system distortions, and resulting feelings that cloud your inner perceptions. They show up as symptoms that may be physical, emotional, mental, or spiritual. Physical pain, illness, depression, sadness, feelings of unworthiness, belief that one is not valuable or lovable, being "stuck" in one's life, frustration over not feeling a purpose for one's life: these are all examples of belief system distortions.

The Story: Don's Excellent Discovery

You would probably like Don: he's a middle-aged man who really likes people. He tells funny stories, and he has a guitar and sings songs. People love to listen to him. Did I mention that he is a rich man? Oh, yes, he really is. He owns a big farm property, and that property is sitting on a huge oil deposit. Millions of dollars' worth of oil lie in that deposit, deep below the ground.

But you'd never know how rich Don is to talk to him. The farm where he lives has an old house that is almost falling down. Don drives an old rickety pickup truck that is barely running. He has no money in the bank and very little cash in his pocket. In fact, as our story begins, Don is upset about his financial situation. Don doesn't know about the oil under the ground, so he doesn't know how rich he is.

In Don's town there is a wise woman known as Ms. Oracle. Since Don is getting desperate about his finances, he goes to Ms. Oracle for advice.

Ms. Oracle tells Don that he doesn't need wealth, because he already has it. "Just get it at home" she says.

Well, Don knows that Ms. Oracle is always correct – so he goes back home to discover all this "wealth."

He starts by looking at the house and barn. He thinks maybe the wealth is money hidden there. For two days he searches and searches – but finds nothing.

"I am a poor person with nothing of value in my house and barn," Don says to himself.

So he goes back to Ms. Oracle.

She says, "Your wealth is more natural. Look at the property itself."

Don decides that perhaps the plants growing on the property represent the wealth she means. So he picks a sample of each different kind of plant that he can find and takes them to town to see if he can sell them. But the man at the plant store says, "You have nothing but weeds here; they are worthless." Don is disappointed and confused. He thinks to himself, "I am a poor person with nothing but worthless plants." Since he's already in town, he goes back to Ms. Oracle.

"Look deeper," she says.

So Don goes back to the property, and looks deeper. Now he sees the earth and dirt that are on the land. Perhaps this dirt is really good topsoil that will grow great plants and even be sold for money to people who want good earth. So he gets his friend from the State Agricultural Association to look at the dirt. "Nope," says his friend, "This is just clay-like, ordinary dirt. That's why nothing is growing here but those weeds."

"Just bad dirt. I'm so poor," is again Don's reaction.

Back to town; back to Ms. Oracle.

"Please give me a little more clarification," says Don.

"The reason you aren't aware of your wealth is because it's covered over with blankets of non-wealthy distortions," says Ms Oracle.

Don goes back home thinking, "O.K., there must be some valuable limestone buried under the worthless dirt. I'll just dig down and find it, then get someone to buy it for a quarry." He goes home and spends the next two weeks digging and digging, but finds no valuable rocks.

By now Don is beginning not to trust Ms. Oracle, so he's pretty insistent. "You tell me that my property has my wealth, you keep saying, 'go deeper'; and I keep running out of money."

Ms. Oracle says, "This is the last time I'll tell you. Be aware of your wealth by going deeper."

"Great," thinks Don, "She says I'm wealthy; but that does me no good because I am not aware of it."

After seeing Ms. Oracle, Don goes to breakfast at the local café and reflects on everything that has been said to him and that he has done. He's looked in the house, at the plants, at the earth, at the rocks; he's found nothing that is wealth.

He decides that the only thing to do is go even deeper, and go through the rocks to see what is underneath.

Of course, you can write the story from here. Don goes under the rocks, finds the oil and finally realizes that he is (and has always been) wealthy.

Moral: Keep digging deeper through the layers of distortions, and your wholeness will emerge.

How Blocks Appear and Where They Go

At the energetic level, these belief system distortions – the "blankets" covering our awareness of wholeness – look like energy blocks, clouds, rips in the energy field, negative patterns that distort the flow of energy, and more.

All of these manifestations change and unbalance the energy field. In repairing or removing them we release energy and clear belief system distortions.

A person may start life with a completely synchronized and totally balanced energy body. As life's small and large traumas occur, distortions, blocks, or "blips" appear in the energy field. The more severe the trauma, the more severe the distortion will be. Breaking an arm would create a large blip; bumping one's leg on a table would cause a lesser one.

Similarly, emotional traumas cause distortions: losing a loved one, for example, would result in a large block, while being startled by a door slamming would create a small one. Distortions of belief systems also cause blocks in the energy field: these blocks occur when the material realm belief system is asked to hold as true those beliefs that violate the actual energetic reality: "I am not worthy;" "all women are sneaky," "people are isolated and have no connection with each other," are examples. Such beliefs appear as rips, blocks, or blips in the energy field.

These various distortions don't coagulate around the type of wound – all physical wounds don't go to one place in the energy field, all emotional wounds to another, etc. Instead, they coalesce around issues and events.

For example, take the issue of abandonment. Donna, a grade-school child, scores poorly on a test, which supports a distortion in the belief system of not being smart enough to deserve attention. On the playground, she doesn't get chosen for either team in the game until last. Now she experiences sadness and rejection, and these emotional traumas cause energy blocks. These energy blocks occur at the same point of the energy body as the belief system distortion.

Perhaps, in her struggle with these feelings of unworthiness, Donna directs and holds the tension of the anticipated abandonment in her neck and shoulders. Soon she starts having pain in the neck and upper back. Once again, these physical blocks will now coalesce at the same point of the energy body.

Like Donna, we may start out working on a physical problem – a painful back, for example – and then find ourselves dealing with emotional difficulties, belief system distortions, or spiritual blocks. Or, the starting point might have been the feelings of unworthiness. The same dynamic operates: as we work with the energy blocks; we might move from the feelings (emotional blocks) to physical or mental distortions, and these in turn would have to be released to resolve the issue.

Often physical curing, or cognitive handling of the emotional issues, operates to release the energy of the blocks in the energy field – we are designed as self-healing mechanisms. You can also start by releasing the energy block, and the body will then heal the physical symptom in the material realm.

Sometimes, merely releasing one won't release the other.

Then, you might need to release the energy block *in addition to* doing the physical curing (the doctor's remedy). In working with energy, I often work with people who are also pursuing an allopathic remedy with a doctor; similarly, I cooperate with cognitive therapy by psychologists and other therapists. Here, the client works with both the energy blocks and the cognitive emotional and belief system issues in the material realm.

Your Block May Be Your Friend

I want to give you a caution here. People often look upon the material realm symptoms and their resultant energy distortions as "negative" or "bad." Indeed, it is hard not to – especially with physical manifestations like chronic pain, rheumatoid arthritis, etc. Yet from an energy standpoint, and from the perspective of seeking an overall healing experience, these blocks are value neutral. They are neither bad nor good – they simply exist.

That may sound like sophistry – and it is certainly a difficult concept when you are in the middle of suffering the physical or emotional effects of these distortions and blocks. At that time, the perspective clearly tends to be the here and now, and it is hard to stand in a larger place. It may be helpful to understand why these blocks exist.

Intention and Purpose

Why do these blocks exist? They protect us when our ego strength is not sufficiently aware to do so. At the core star realm we understand the connectedness and wholeness of being part of the light. At the intention realm, we have a purpose that creates more beauty in the universe, and that purpose always tends to move us more closely and clearly into the light, into the direction of unity.

When we are born into the material world as human physical beings, however, we are unprotected and unaware of how to stay safe. A part of us (usually referred to as the ego) is assigned the task of keeping us safe. That part quickly perceives that "other" is bigger, stronger, and more mobile, and that "other" is or may be a threat. The way of staying safe is to stay "separate" from "other."

From an energetic perspective, "separate" is somewhat of an illusion; however, from the material realm perspective, it is a key to survival. From that perspective, part of us keeps us safe by keeping us separate – moving away from the unity. We learn to do this by looking at what we learn from parents, from culture, from our environment.

All of these mechanisms of separation stop or impede the free flow of energy and block the perceived threat posed by unity.

It's important to remember that our defenses and material realm blocks serve a legitimate purpose.

Imagine a toddler going out into the back yard. The neighbor's dog is about as tall as the toddler; also, big kids up the street might hurt the toddler when playing ball – so we put up a fence to keep all those threats out.

Now our toddler is a teenager. She'd like to pet the neighbor's dog and play with the kids up the street. But the fence is still there – only now it's imprisoning her instead of protecting her.

So it is with our defenses and material realm mechanisms for separation. They were created to keep us separate in the best way we knew how at the time. They may have now outlived their usefulness, and we are ready to let go of them. With an attitude of gratefulness for their origins and once-useful purposes, we are now ready to move these "fences" out of our system.

The blocks do not cease to exist when we move them; they may be transformed into a different energy or released to a different place in our bigger energy field. They will no longer block the creative energy flow and cause negative symptoms. Because they sometimes remain a part of us (though no longer blocking energy), it is important to adopt and accept their quality as being a part of our wholeness, *and not a negative interruption to it.*

Why Keep Our Blocks?

Much of reclaiming our wholeness is a process of reassuring and convincing that "guardian" part of ourselves that we do know what we're doing, and that it is safe to let go of the devices that hinder us from the free flow of energy. In the example of the teenager wanting to take down the fence (her block), she must convince her "guardian" that she is, in fact, big enough to protect herself from the dog, and that she can hold her own with the other teenagers with whom she wishes to play. And she may still be unsure as to whether or not she will be safe with the other kids.

We may have that emotional reluctance, even though the manifestation of the block on the material realm is something we clearly want to get rid of. We tell ourselves, "I don't want the pain." To say instead, "I trust that I won't use my pain-free state to get me into even bigger trouble" – that's the one that challenges us.

On the other hand, since the connection with wholeness happens at the deepest level of our being, and then radiates out into our day-to-day world, I often see clients who become open in a new way when they connect to wholeness. Suddenly the next book they read, or the next counselor they see, or the next concepts they study become the key for them to really expand their life.

The awareness and connection with wholeness occurred in the deepest level – it now can seek a translation at the more surface levels of our belief systems and emotions. The books, counselors, ways we think, and ways we feel, are all appropriate forums to make that translation to our day-to-day lives.

In the second window, we realize that the reason for not experiencing our wholeness is our belief system's distortions and blocks. The purpose of this window is to clear the way to allow the emotional body at the material realm to let go of those "blankets" and endorse the wholeness.

This is a two-fold process. First, you need to understand your individual blocks. Second, you need to allow the possibility of their release emotionally.

You probably have no difficulty in listing your blocks – their symptoms (emotional or physical pain, eruptions of anger, feelings of self-doubt, etc.) cause you to seek healing in your life.

You may have more difficulty in seeing how these symptoms or blocks might serve you (now or in the past) in a positive way, as well as have a negative impact on you. Consider these examples:

a) At the same time a hurt back is causing pain, it may also provide an acceptable reason to refrain from doing some unpleasant task;

b) A person's anger, while causing huge negative difficulties, may also provide an energizing feeling and a sense of power and aliveness;

c) Believing yourself unworthy may motivate you to try hard, thus producing a positive result.

When you see the positive it's easier to incorporate all of your experience into your wholeness – without having to get rid of some of "you" in order to be whole.

Right now, you don't need to be able to define the positive aspects of your specific blocks; the question here will be whether you can sense that a block does provide some positive impact.

The first half of the Second Window Energy Tool is about your blocks. The second half relates to another dynamic that occurs in transforming our energy bodies: we like to stay as we are.

In the material realm we recognize a law of physics that states, "A body at rest tends to remain at rest, and a body in motion tends to remain in motion." This striving for the status quo is also true in our energy bodies. I sometimes describe it by referring to my experience growing up in the country. During the spring rains, the dirt roads became quite muddy, and as people drove on the roads, ruts developed. The ruts became deep, and after the roads dried, the ruts stayed. You would be driving along, then fall into the rut. It was difficult to stay up where you wanted to be on the road.

Our energy bodies are the same way. You have spent your entire life, until now, running your energy system to develop the patterns it holds. Those patterns create "ruts" in your energy system. As you make changes there is a "rubber-band" effect; you make a change, but fall back into the rut. To complete the metaphor, by completing this Energy Tool, you will "grade the energy road," much as road workers graded those dirt roads in the late spring.

Energy Tool: Opening the Second Window

This is a powerful self-healing method for you to reinforce the lesson of the second window and increase the experience of wholeness in your life. This Energy Tool is in two parts, but ideally both parts should be completed in one sitting, so allow plenty of time.

Part One

1. Get some blank paper and a pen or pencil. Find a quiet place. If you like, put on some

reflective music – preferably something without lyrics.

2. Spend a few minutes just paying attention to your breathing, quieting your mind, and letting yourself relax and focus on listening to the nothingness of the most-quiet place in your mind.

3. Take the pen and paper and list each thing you think of that is an interruption or block to your experience of your wholeness: this will include physical conditions and symptoms, feelings, emotions, beliefs, ideas; whatever interrupts or blocks you. Number each item, and give each block or interruption a separate number, on a separate line.

4. When you are finished, spend a few minutes reflecting on how these blocks interrupt your experience of your wholeness; place an "x" beside any of the items listed that you conclude don't actually interrupt or diminish your experience of wholeness.

5. Now, please review the list again: this time consider each item on the list, one at a time, and see if you can imagine or understand what positive purpose or reason this item might serve or have served for you. This is not to attempt to find a reason to keep it; this is so you can see if you can understand, or even make up, a legitimate positive service this may have provided for you or may still provide for you. With each item that you can

find a legitimate positive response, place a check mark by the item.

6. Now take a separate sheet of paper and write down any items from the first sheet that do not have either an "x" or a check mark. This is your "A" list of blocks, your greatest opportunity for transformation. If you don't have any that have neither an "x" nor a check mark: leave the sheet blank and save it with the other.

7. Please take both sheets of paper you have generated, and save them along with the pieces of paper from the first exercise.

Part Two

8. You are now ready for the second part of this exercise. You may want to take a break for a few minutes. When you are ready, get in a comfortable position, and once again spend a few minutes quieting your mind, paying attention to your breathing and letting yourself relax and focus on listening to the nothingness of the most-quiet place in your mind.

9. You are now going to "bathe" your energy body, and clear out those energy ruts, so that in the future you can make the transformations you want more lasting, without as much of the rubber band effect causing the changes not to hold.

10. Visualize a clear blue cleansing light; make your bar of soap of that light, and make the water that light. So you now have soap and water of that clear blue cleansing light. The next part of the exercise you can do either by placing your hands on your body in the parts indicated, or by visualizing the movements in your mind

    a. Physically start at your feet, and "wash" the blue soap and water into your feet, ankles, and up your legs; through your torso, arms, hands, neck, and up through your head – in other words imagine yourself filling your entire body with this blue light and let it cleanse and clear the surface and into the middle of your body – so that as you progress up the body, the parts you have washed retain a clear blue filling with light. The physical motions should be just as you wash yourself, but with great care and tenderness – don't force the blue light into your field, but allow it to gently infuse itself into your body as you make the rhythmic washing movements with your hands. When you have completed the entire process, you will have a body that is "wet" with blue light – all the way from top to bottom, front to back, side to side, and inside and out.

    b. Visualize a towel that is fluffy and warm and soft. It is rose colored – rose is the color of unconditional love. With the same attention to detail, dry yourself with the rose-colored towel, allowing the rose color to infuse itself into your body from the towel.

11. When you have completed the process, once again sit and simply feel the clear, fresh, open, cleansed energy body. Close with whatever reflections you have about the exercise – and with an expression of appreciation to your total being for having the willingness to do this process.

Thank you for your participation.

CHAPTER 9

THE THIRD WINDOW: WITHIN YOU THE KNOWLEDGE ALREADY EXISTS AS TO HOW TO CLEAR UP THE DISTORTIONS

The Story: Buddy Builds a Nest

It was springtime in the forest and time for all the animals to get ready for the summer. Our hero today is Buddy, the bird. This was the third year that Buddy and his wife Bertie had been married, and Buddy woke up knowing it was time to build the nest. Buddy was eager to get started because the nest he built the year before had been praised by all the other birds as being one of the best they'd ever seen.

"This year, I'll build a neater, cleaner, bigger, better nest than ever!" Buddy promised Bertie.

Buddy had a disturbing thought. "What if I can't remember how to build a nest?" The more Buddy thought about it, the worse it got. He couldn't remember exactly what he used for the nest, where he found the straw – "Or was it straw? – maybe it was sticks?" The more he thought, the more blocked he got. He couldn't remember the size, the shape, the color – he couldn't remember anything at all about nest-building.

Buddy panicked. "Oh my gosh," he thought, "If I can't build the nest, we won't have a home for the chicks. Everything will be ruined!!!"

By now, Buddy had not only forgotten how to build the nest, he also had become so upset that he almost couldn't think at all.

He was so ashamed. "I can't tell any of the other birds about this; they would just laugh at me."

Then Buddy had an idea. He would get advice on how to go about building a home for his family. And he knew just who he could ask: the animal kingdom's expert, Mr. Big Bear.

Buddy flew to the side of the mountain at the edge of the forest where he found Mr. Bear. Mr. Bear was just arising from his winter's nap and was stretching and yawning as he awoke.

"Oh hello, Buddy, how are you?"

"To tell the truth, Mr. Bear, I'm not so good," Buddy replied. "You see, I've forgotten how to build my home for my family, and I'm very worried and scared that I won't get it done; so I'm here to ask for advice."

"Buddy, Buddy, Buddy," said Mr. Bear, "You're not thinking clearly. You don't build a home; you just find a nice cave. That's what we bears do."

"Thanks for the help." And Buddy flew off to find a cave.

But there were no caves in the forest near where he wanted to have his family. "This just isn't working. I'd better get some more advice," thought Buddy. "I'd better go ask my friend Joey the Beaver: he's always building his home."

So Buddy flew back into the forest and found Joey cutting down a tree with his teeth.

"Joey, I have a problem. I can't remember how to build our home for the summer."

Joey stopped gnawing on the tree and looked at Buddy. "That's easy, Buddy. You start by cutting down some trees (or in your case – since you don't need anything so big – you can cut down twigs). Then you use those materials to start building."

"Thank you, thank you. I'll get started right away." And Buddy flew back to the area where he wanted to build a nest. He tried using his beak to cut down a very little tree – but his beak wouldn't cut through the tree.

"Well," thought Buddy, "Other animals' solutions don't seem to work for birds. I guess I'll have to admit to at least one bird that I don't know how to build a nest."

So Buddy went back to Bertie, and confessed to her.

"I started thinking, and planning, and then all of a sudden I got worried. I got blocked in remembering how to start building a nest; then I couldn't remember what materials to use or how to put them together; then I started worrying about what would happen if I didn't remember; then I started being ashamed because birds are supposed to know; then I got more afraid that I wouldn't ever remember again. I asked two experts, but

I couldn't use the advice they gave me. I don't know what to do."

Buddy paced back and forth on the branch.

"Bertie, do you think I ought to enroll in some nest-building course? Do I have time before we need the nest? Do you think I ought to find some kind of pill to take to make me less afraid? What shall I do and who should I go to for learning how to build this nest???"

Bertie was a very wise bird. She gave Buddy a hug and said, "Buddy, all you need to do is relax. Building nests is what birds do. I want you to go over there and take a nap. And when you wake up, don't plan or think; just start building the nest."

Well, Buddy didn't know what she was talking about exactly, but he was pretty tired from all of his anxious thoughts, so he lay down and took a nice nap.

When he woke up, he started building the nest.

He found himself flying through the air, picking up some sticks and straw, bringing them back to a crook in the tree and putting them together into a beautiful nest. Suddenly he realized that he knew exactly what he was doing.

And from that moment forward, Buddy worked like a beaver, and with the strength of a bear, but he did what a bird does: he built the neatest, cleanest, biggest, best nest that anyone ever saw!

Moral: Within us, the knowledge already exists as to how to clear up the distortions.

Implementing the Mind/Body Connection

You know how to clear up the distortions and accomplish your own healing. You may not yet, however, have access to that knowledge. If you can just understand and accept this wonderful facet of yourself, you will have prepared your physical body for the living in wholeness that you are moving into.

This step is about clearing and preparing the physical body at the material realm for living from a place of wholeness. Most people find it particularly challenging to access the ability to heal and live from wholeness where the complaints are physical illness, injury, or pain. Those physical symptoms seem too mechanical to be influenced by our beliefs or our intention.

On the other hand, we do understand that there is a huge mind/body connection involved in physical disease. We've all known of people who have had "spontaneous remissions" of serious illnesses; we've seen how mental and emotional stress seem to cause pains, such as ulcers, headaches, etc. It takes no leap of faith to understand that if we can cause illness, then we can similarly cause healing.

I make the assumption that "wholeness" will bring about "healing." We need to take a moment to look at that.

Healing is More Than "Curing"

When you decided to come into physical life, you had a lot of choices to make about qualities, tendencies, characteristics, temperament, physical body type, race, gender, etc. All of these choices would affect your experience and none of these traits were taken by accident.

You could have been a short fat girl with one foot deformed, or

You could have been a 6'4" boy with strong muscles and an appetite for physical exercise.

Even if you put them both in the same family, their life experiences will be totally different.

Just for fun, on the sole basis of the information above: ask yourself, "Which of these two siblings is happier?"

You probably answer that the boy would likely be.

Now add the additional information that the girl has an optimistic, jolly outlook, and always has from the time she was baby.

Her brother, on the other hand, was always a worrier, was always concerned that he wouldn't have enough, and was always afraid. .

Now, ask yourself again, "Which one is happier?"

The point is that you can add any other traits – intelligence, beauty, self confidence, quick temper, chronic depression, chronic pain in the neck, etc, and get completely different effects. Yet each person is the same essence. Beneath all of the characteristics, traits, and qualities, each person is a being of light, a connected, integral piece of the universe.

Each has more or less "forgotten" that core, or is unable to reach it.

"Healing" is not fixing the chronic pain, or curing the depression, or taking the weight off. "Healing" is the process/act of going underneath those outside/inside items and going to the essence – the core.

It is remembering and becoming aware of that divine essence of light that is who you already really were, then letting your consciousness connect and settle there, and then living from that place of awareness.

Your depression will obviously be gone – or it won't.

Your pain will be gone – or it won't.

Ultimately, those matters will not determine whether or not you are healed. In other words, there is a distinction between "curing" a physical problem, and healing it.

If you could cure a headache with a pill, and in the process allow yourself to ignore a more serious problem indicated by the headache (a brain tumor, for example), curing that symptom will not be a healing.

Sometimes, healing means keeping the symptom for a while in order to derive what we need to receive from it.

"Healed" will feel full – it may not feel happy, or comfortable, or easy – yet it cannot help but feel joyful, open, confident, and eager to meet the next event, time, person, and day.

Healing is a matter of the perspective with which we perceive our physical difficulties. Suppose we're like a finger with a splinter in it, with that finger's limited perspective. We want the pain to stop. From that "finger-perspective," if we see the other hand coming with a great big old needle, and proposing to tear into our skin even more – right at the place where we're already sore – that does NOT look like healing. It looks like some sadistic ritual.

Yet from our perspective as a total body, we know the way to bring about healing is to take the splinter out, even though in the short term it might cause more pain.

When you come from the perspective of wholeness, you have the vantage point of a larger person than either the finger or the personality caught with the physical pain in your life. Without diminishing the suffering, you can see that the issue of the physical disease is a "red car/blue car" issue. Wholeness may lead to its being cured – in fact it does much more often than it doesn't. But in the larger perspective it does not have to be cured to be "healed."

I was given a dramatic learning experience of this principle during my senior year of classes at the energy healing school I attended. At the end of a week of class, a group of us went out to dinner together, to a Mexican restaurant near the school. There were ten of us seated around a central long table in the small dining room. Six tables for two or four people surrounded us.

While we were waiting for our food to come, WHAM! I heard the sound of a person landing on the floor.

"Roger! Roger!!" A woman screamed. Just across from me a man lay motionless on the floor. When I looked at him, I immediately saw a big line of energy up the neck into the head. There was also a big black hole in the energy at his heart. A part of me was stunned, and a part was amazed that I could realize from the energy I perceived that he was having a stroke and heart attack.

Our table was immediately shoved to the wall. Those of us on my side of the table were stuck standing between the wall and the table. We used techniques to hold positive energy for the people on the other side of the table, but we were physically confined. On the other side, a student who was also a nurse started CPR. Two other students started doing energy work.

In a very short time, the EMT's were there – working on him. During the whole time, his wife kept yelling: "Roger, Roger, don't you leave me!" "Roger, stay; I need you." While the work was going on, I saw him come up out of his body – hover for a bit, and as his wife continued to implore him, went back in.

A few minutes later, however, he came out of his body again. This time he was assured, seemed to know that he was not going back, and moved over just behind his wife as she watched the emergency work being done on him.

With my eyes I saw a wisp – like a floating, vertical piece of dental floss; with my "inside eyes" – the mind screen on which I see some energy – I could recognize him. It was as if his face, head and upper body were floating in the exact place that I was seeing the "wisp." It was now clear that he knew that he was to go; that he was offering support to his wife (even though she was probably not consciously aware of it), and that he would not be revived. Shortly after that the EMT's took him out on a gurney, followed by his wife and the other couple that had been at their table. As his spirit followed behind them, he stopped, turned around, and gave a nod of recognition and appreciation to those of us who had been holding and working energy.

We formed a circle in the space where the EMT's had been working and invited the other patrons to join us in offering positive thoughts and prayers for those involved.

I sat back down in my chair, trying to absorb the profound events I had witnessed. I understood that he was dead (which was confirmed when he was pronounced DOA at the hospital), and I also understood that it was what he was supposed to be doing at the time. It was clear that the death was not an "end" of him, but a transition to something else, and that there was some purpose that it served for him, for his wife, and even for the rest of us in the restaurant.

"Curing" would have involved recovering from the attack; doing what his soul was meant to do at that moment – which did not "cure" him – was the "healing" experience for all of us.

The question of what is "healed" also carries over into the emotional and belief systems. Some say that we need to be healed from fear. But even if we are totally healthy, a truck bearing down on us will cause fear. That's what fear is for: to inform us of danger. "Healed" – in that moment and in that circumstance – will look fearful. In fact, not having fear under that circumstance would be an unhealed denial of reality.

Or you might think you would not be sad, or angry, if you were healed. What about sitting in a hospital emergency room with a small child that an adult has just brutalized? The child is hurt and crying, and you also see the abuser walking through the room. "Healed" in that situation may well see you feeling sad, sorry, and angry.

The distortions that separate you from wholeness keep you unhealed. When you consider the above examples, you can see that you knew what "healed" was – innately. You also knew innately how to achieve that state.

Healing as a Positive Adventure

We heal ourselves by finding that powerful, whole person inside, and living from there. Since that whole person is covered over with the blocks and distortions that come from our past experiences, we mis-perceive healing to be from the current place to remove distortions. The negative aspect of "removing distortions" replaces the positive goal of living from an already-healed place.

Unfortunately, that doesn't work very well. Instead, we seek a transformation where the person can live from a place of completeness. But the personality having the distortions experiences him/herself as flawed. That's not a person who has the power to bring about the transformation desired.

Living From the Core Essence

Near the heart area deep in your energy body is the core essence of your personality – it appears as a light of very high vibration. It is the fastest point of energy vibration in your energy body. Around this core essence the rest of the auric body is formed.

Each person has a slightly different core essence vibration, which creates different color patterns. Like snowflakes, I've seen no two core essences that are identical. The colors seem to relate to the basic highest qualities of that individual. For example, a core essence that is primarily rose light relates to a person whose basic nature is full of unconditional love. Purple is a very spiritual color, green relates to adventuring, growing and learning, etc. Each person's core essence tends to be a combination of colors (in fact, all colors of the spectrum are in each core essence to some degree).

When people can live from their core essence, they experience a feeling of wholeness. However, distortions cover the core essence like blankets. The distortions have a lower vibration, appear to be thick, and keep the person from a consistent experience of their higher-self qualities.

You are learning to bring that higher vibration of the core essence into the physical body and into the energy field, and then to hold it there, even while the distortions remain. You will bring the most positive powerful aspect of the energy out past the lower-vibration distortions.

Once the higher vibration is held out in the physical body and the energy fields, as well as in the core essence, the energy blocks and distortions have less impact. Because they are a lower vibration, and because they are now surrounded by the higher vibration, they have a tendency to dissolve. Energetically, you have now positioned yourself to experience being in a healed state. In the material realm, then, you will experience life differently.

In the Energy Tool at the end of this chapter, you will have your first experience of feeling the power of that core essence. Remember that you are involved in a seven-step process; the experience may or may not have a powerful impact. Treat this step as a game: play with it; play it; and don't worry about the efficacy at this point. Be like Buddy the Bird: relax and follow your instincts.

No matter what your mind does with it, the experience of it holds the foundation for changing your experience of yourself in your life.

Energy Tool: Opening the Third Window

This is a self-healing method for you to reinforce this concept in your material physical body and provide a fertile ground for increasing the experience of wholeness in your life.

1. Find a quiet place; if you like, put on some reflective music – preferably something without lyrics.

2. Spend a few minutes just paying attention to your breathing, quieting your mind, and letting yourself relax and focus on listening to the nothingness of the most-quiet place in your mind.

3. Bring both hands to a point in the middle of your chest, just an inch or so above the nipples, and point all of your fingers straight into the middle of your body at that point.

4. Extend your fingers with energy fingers that come into the exact middle of your chest (if you don't feel this extension, visualize or imagine it); at the same time concentrate

on breathing to the exact point where your fingers will intersect the center of your chest.

5. Visualize your energy fingers moving through layer after layer of clouded energy, and sticky energy, and low vibration, dense energy: keep breathing to the exact center; and then see/experience your fingers coming to the exact place where your breathe intersects them. Here you will feel a point of incredibly high vibration – concentrated in about the size of a quarter, but three dimensional. This vibration will feel energized, vibrant, yet profoundly caring and healthy. You may see the colors of it; if you don't, just imagine the most consistent color with your health and well-being – and let that color be the focus of your visual experience. If you feel or see nothing, keep breathing to that point and repeat the process of bringing your energy fingers from the physical fingers, through the layers, and to the point where it intersects with your breath. (If you still feel or see nothing, create an image of what it would look like, and create the exercise as a visualization – with or without a sense of actual perceiving).

6. When you have connected fully with the core essence vibration, let that fast, healthy vibration move through your energy fingers (as if they were tunnels to your physical hands), and let that fast vibration expand

into and fill your hands with the same vibration. You are moving the energy by intention, so there is no effort involved. Feel and experience that exact high vibration from the middle of your chest in both of your hands as they continue to point into your chest.

7. Now, keeping that vibration in your hands, place your hands on each area of your physical body where you have physical challenges of any kind, and at each place allow the vibration from your hands to expand and go specifically to the points of physical challenge (if you are experiencing this high vibration energy as a particular color, it may be helpful to see the color going in at the same time as the feeling of the energy vibration). Keep your hands at each point long enough so that you feel the vibration expanded from your hands into that place. (If you ever feel like you are losing touch with the vibration in your hands, take one of your hands back to your chest, and refresh the connection and the experiencing of the vibration).

8. When you have filled each place of physical challenge, bring both hands back to your chest, and again refresh the connection, and experience of the vibration in them.

9. Finally, keeping the vibration in your hands, place your hands on top of your head, and

expand the vibration into your head, and then bring that vibration down throughout your entire physical body. Feel the vibration of your body at that level. Let that vibration (and color) infuse itself into your entire physical body.

10. Now bring your hands back to your heart, with the palms over your heart.

11. When you have completed the process, once again sit and simply feel your physical body. Close with whatever reflections you have about the exercise – and with an expression of appreciation to the total being that is you for having the willingness to do this process.

Thank you for your participation.

CHAPTER 10

THE FOURTH WINDOW: ALIGNING WITH THE INTENTION TO RECOGNIZE YOUR WHOLENESS IS THE FIRST STEP

Now is the moment when you make a conscious choice. If you are going to open yourself to the changes, and truly set the intention for wholeness, it will come with this fourth window.

The Story: The Magic Beam

Once upon a long place from now in a faraway time, there lived a little girl named Dawn. Dawn was a very intelligent young lady; full of life, and well liked by her friends and family. She lived in a small town on the edge of the woods, and loved to go out and play in the woods.

Wait! Before we tell you more about Dawn, there are some things you will want to know about her kingdom. This place looked very much like the world you are living in, but there was one big difference. For every person, there was also a magic beam of light that came out of the sky and went into the earth. This beam was about as big around as a telephone pole and followed the person around wherever they went. The magic beam was very beautiful; but it was only visible when you wore special glasses. Without the glasses it was an invisible magic beam of light.

While we tell this story, we are giving you a pair of the special glasses, so you now can see the magic beams of light.

Now look around at the people of Dawn's village. See all the people, and see all the magic beams of light – one going with each person.

Sometimes people had the beam of light going right through them – it came in at the head and went straight down coming out just between their feet. Those people looked pretty happy, were usually pleasant, and seemed to know what they were supposed to be doing, and how to do it. This is not surprising, for the magic beam carried in it the information that let people know just those things.

For other people the beam of light was farther away. Sometimes it was about two feet away beside them, and didn't touch them at all, except that once in a while a little offshoot of light from the magic beam jumped out and connected with the person. The rest of the time, the people were just walking along with the beam of light beside them, or behind them. These people had a hard time knowing exactly what to do. Often they felt kind of frustrated and dissatisfied.

How did this happen?

When people were born, they were given the magic beam of light to guide them in their lives. But it was not totally connected. Since the beam was invisible, many people in the kingdom didn't even believe it existed.

The First Person didn't know about it. When he wanted to find out what to do and how to do it, he started by thinking, and studying. Other people came, and he listened to them. Then he went to school. And all of these things moved the invisible magic beam around – and finally, it happened to bring the beam directly overhead, and First Person ended up connected to it. As soon as he connected completely to it, and it came down through the center of his body, he felt the purpose and knowing of what he was to do. Since he didn't see the beam as a beam of light, he thought this "knowing" and "connection" came as a result of all the work he did. Well, he wasn't entirely wrong – but the work didn't give him the connection. Instead, the work was what allowed him to bring the beam into him, and the beam gave him the connection.

So everybody in the kingdom was taught to study and think and go to school. These were good things to do; but they didn't necessarily get people connected with their invisible magic beam of light; only those people who happened to step under the beam as it was moving around got connected. For the majority, however, the beam continued to move around, but didn't connect directly with them.

Now let's go back to Dawn. Dawn was about two feet to the right of her magic beam (we know that because we have the glasses), but a couple of off-shoots of purple light from the beam came coursing across the span and connected with Dawn's heart. Dawn didn't know about the light – but she did know that she had this IDEA. Her idea was that she wanted to make friends with the wild animals of the forest, so they would trust her and she could serve them.

It was more of a feeling for her than a knowing. "I love animals, and I want to know them better, and I want them to know me," is how she said it.

So one morning Dawn went to the forest, sat down and called the animals to her. They didn't come. She saw a rabbit and started to talk to it and walk toward it, but he runs away. She saw a deer; sat very still, and asked the deer to come to her, but it was afraid and ran away. None of the animals made friends with Dawn.

Morning after morning this happened in just the same way, so Dawn decided to ask for help.

She went to First Person and asked. He said she must go to school and learn all about the animals and then she would be able to make friends with them.

Dawn went to school and learned all about the animals; then she went back to the woods. But still none of the animals made friends with her.

Dawn went to her best friend, Sue, and told her the problem. Sue said, "Well, if they won't make friends with you, then it is just not supposed to be. You must find something else to do besides making friends with the animals."

Dawn tried to follow Sue's advice. But do you remember the two purple shoots of light from the beam that were connecting with Dawn's heart? That connection kept reminding her that she was to make friends with the wild animals of the forest.

Dawn was not very happy. In the center of the village lived a woman who was considered the wisest person in the world. Dawn went to her.

"Wise Woman, how can I get the animals to make friends with me?"

"Dawn," says the woman, "You must bring the magic beam directly into you"

Dawn says, "I want to be friends with the animals from the bottom of my heart, so I must be doing that."

"You are not talking about the beam, my Dear," the Wise Woman says, "That's desire. Desire can be a good thing; it helps motivate you to your purpose. But it is not the magic beam. Align with the beam."

Dawn thought, "What does she mean by 'the beam'?"

So Dawn went back to the woods and said, "I am creating the magic beam to come directly through me. I want it to come through me now." Then she invited the animals.

Nothing different happened.

In another conversation with the Wise Woman, she told Dawn, "You don't create the magic beam; it's already there; it's something you align with."

Dawn was very confused.

She went back to the woods, and thought: "Well, maybe I could treat the animals as if they were already friends." She pretended that she was friends already, and acted like there was a circle and the rabbit and deer came to her.

But nothing different happened.

The Wise Woman said, "Now you are trying to create the outcome. How the animals feel toward you is not your responsibility. Whether or not they make friends with you is up to them. Your job is to control how you are toward the animals – to be, feel, and do the things that express your friendship for them. Don't focus on the 'outcome.' Align with the magic beam, and all will follow."

Poor Dawn was so frustrated she didn't know what to do.

Finally Wise Woman said, "Dawn, sit down and put on these magic glasses." When Dawn did, she saw the beam of light just two feet to the right of her. It was so beautiful! Dawn gently allowed herself and the beam to merge so that the beam went completely through her.

As soon as she did, Dawn felt different. She had a sense that the animals needed to trust her in order for her to help them.

Now the magic beam was running right through her all the time. When she went back to the woods, she again went to a clearing and saw the rabbit. But this time the rabbit was attracted and reassured by the beautiful energy, and came right to Dawn. The deer came, too.

Dawn ended up with many animals as friends. We will leave to another time the story of how Dawn came to help the animals.

Aligning With Intent

Until this point, we have been working with energy to prepare the mental, emotional, and physical bodies for the changes. Now we move to a deeper level. The first three windows are the preparation of the field – plowing, watering, and working the soil of your self. Now we start the planting and growing process.

Beneath the distortions you have an intention to be aware of your wholeness. In the energy realm, however, your distorted connection causes you to connect instead with a self-perception of being flawed. In this window you accomplish clearing of that distorted connection by aligning with the underlying intention.

Aligning an intention is the energy equivalent to changing the physical structure. Just as the doctor needs to set the bone, to allow the fracture to heal itself in an aligned manner, you need to have an intention that is correctly aligned in order to manifest the healed result.

How the Energy Realm Works

The energy realm differs in properties from the material. In the material realm, you move about physically in a geographical manner. If you want to go to the other side of the room, you walk there. In the energy realm, you move by intention. If you want to be on the other side of the room, you *intend* to be there, and you are there.

Intention is the "physical" part of the energy realm, and holds the framework for the rest of the energetic aspects of a person. Before moving to the healing of the emotional and mental resistance to wholeness (5th and 6th windows), a correct alignment with the intention is critical.

Honoring the Mystery

Aligning an intention is a serious matter. We must honor the "mystery" of the universe. When we try to discover what our underlying intent is, there is always a problem of perspective. We have the danger that we are setting the intent from the perspective of the "finger" instead of from the "whole body," that what we ask for would be the opposite of what is healing for us from the larger perspective. We can, however, trust that our bigger/wiser self knows what is in our best interest.

To avoid that danger, whenever I align an intention for myself, or for someone else, I pre-qualify it to include the higher self's perspective: *"If* it's in the client's best and highest interest, I align with the intention to..." (then state the matter intended). In that manner, I avoid working at cross purposes with myself or with my client.

Even as we move now to align with the intention for your wholeness, we'll be careful to honor the possibility that now is not the best time from the perspective of your highest self.

The universe is very literal: it is important to phrase the intention properly. One person set an intention "to try to successfully complete a particular course of study." She didn't complete it and "tried" again. Unfortunately, when she intends to "try," the universe honors that, and leaves her in the position of "trying" – not succeeding.

Similarly, setting an intention by saying "I want..." sets an intention for being in the state of wanting, not in the state of having accomplished. So we pay attention to what we state as our intention.

And what is the intention that will clear this level of the energy realm for living in our wholeness?

The statement I like is, "to hold the core essence vibration in my body and my energy field, and to hold the awareness of it in my consciousness." I see it as a two-part change: (1) to keep the wholeness throughout the entire body and energy field, and (2) to remain aware of it from moment to moment.

Energy Tool: Opening the Fourth Window

This is a self-healing method for you to align your intention toward wholeness.

1. Find a quiet place; and, if you like put on some reflective music – preferably something without lyrics.

2. Spend a few minutes just paying attention to your breathing, quieting your mind, and letting yourself relax and focus on listening to the nothingness of the most-quiet place in your mind.

3. Review in your mind what living in awareness of wholeness and living from that place of wholeness might mean in your life – what is your perception of your wholeness now?

4. Decide if you are willing to open yourself to all the differences of experience you may have – positive and negative – if you live from the place of wholeness.

5. If so, decide that you will now make that choice in your life.

6. Take your hands, and once again connect with your core essence, as you did before, by extending energy fingers into the center of your chest, assimilating the vibration of your core essence, and bringing that vibration out into your hands.

7. Hold your hands with the core essence vibration on top of your head, and let that vibration come out of your hands and down through your entire body.

8. When you have completed, bring your hands back to your heart, with the palms over your heart.

9. While holding that vibration in your body, state aloud,

"If it's in my best and highest interest, I align with the intention to hold the core essence vibration in my body and my energy field, and to hold the awareness of it in my consciousness."

10. Think about the meanings of both parts of the intention statement; then repeat the statement aloud, while holding in your

consciousness the sincerity and positive decision to carry this intention forward.

11. When you have completed the process, once again sit and simply feel your physical body. Close with whatever reflections you have about the exercise – and with an expression of appreciation to the total being that is you for having the willingness to do this process.

Thank you for your participation.

CHAPTER 11

THE FIFTH WINDOW: YOU DON'T HAVE TO CHANGE TO BE WHOLE

This proposition sounds easy – it sounds like something we already believe. But it becomes one of the hardest to incorporate into our experience. Although we might believe it, we don't live it.

The Story: Dwight the Bear

Dwight lived out towards the edge of the forest, where he could easily find caves for his long winter's naps; but close enough in that there were lots of good shrubs, leaves, and, of course, honey for a satisfying diet.

When we first see him, Dwight is a grown-up, but a young grown-up among the bears. And he was so happy! But he didn't even think about whether he's happy or not – he just knew it.

He would wake up in the morning eagerly anticipating whatever might happen that day; go and do whatever he did. Without thinking he just knew what was next to do. When he was hungry he found something to eat. Sometimes, when he was down at the river fishing, he felt like playing, and he jumped in the water and splashed around. This didn't do his fishing any good; but he just giggled and roared and had a great time. The other animals would sometimes join in; or not. If they didn't, he had fun by himself; if they did, he really enjoyed playing with them.

One summer, Dwight was fooling around near the water and severely hurt his right hind leg – so that it gave him a lot of pain and he couldn't do a lot of the things that he normally did. So Dwight just did what he could do, and filled his day with the activities that he could accomplish while limping. He was still the same happy, optimistic bear.

Dwight never thought about how he looked, or what his "path" was – he just lived. He knew what he would do when he did it; was connected to a sense of rightness about what he did and when he acted. Towards fall, he would eat a lot of extra food, then find a place to sleep. His body felt sleepy; so he went to a place that would be warm (usually a cave), and fell asleep. When he was done sleeping he woke up – to find it was spring – and boy, was he hungry. Whenever Dwight woke up, he was eager to see what the day would bring.

Then he would spend another active spring and summer, enjoying his life.

But one fine spring day that all changed! Dwight was put into the most challenging period of his life.

It started innocently enough. Dwight's friend Ollie the Otter was playing on the bank of the river, and was where some people had camped out. He found a mirror that they left behind.

Ollie thought that the mirror was pretty interesting – the way the colors of the sun changed direction when they hit the shiny glass – and he gave it to Dwight as a present.

Dwight spent a day or so looking at the mirror – when all of a sudden it dawned on him that the mirror showed him what a bear looked like – specifically, it showed him what Dwight the bear looked like.

Dwight had never even thought of that as a question before – "What do I look like?" Had it stopped there it would probably not have been a big deal. But it didn't

Dwight thought a lot of thoughts he hadn't had before. How he first saw himself was probably what bears are supposed to look like. But he noticed that it was different from his father – who was the strongest bear he ever knew – and Dwight noticed that he wasn't as well-muscled as his father. So Dwight started to be a little ashamed of how he didn't measure up.

Well, it went on from there. After he noticed what he was supposed to look like, he started realizing that there were other ways he didn't measure up – so he started trying to figure out how to fix them. Instead of that happening, though, it just got worse. As summer progressed Dwight started his yearly pattern of eating more – but this time, he had the mirror to show him how fat he was getting. Oh, my gosh! Now he's totally fat – he'll have to get that fat off before he can relax and play with the other bears again – they'd laugh at that silly body.

Then he started to realize that before he could play with them, he'd have to hide and get his body fixed. But when he went off by himself, it didn't feel right – and so he started being sad and feeling disconnected and isolated. And the part of him that said, go play now – had to be ignored, because Dwight was working on fixing his body; but just the fact of ignoring that urge to follow what his inside voice told him to do, caused him to be more disconnected.

So he started talking to himself with an inside voice that wouldn't be fooled by that "go play" voice. He kept saying, "Dwight, you can't be seen looking like this; you'll be ok when you get your body shape back; but you're just being undisciplined and lazy about diet and exercise; do you want to be fat and ugly and unacceptable? You're so stupid; you know what to do and you just don't do it."

But instead of feeling better, all of these corrections he was offering himself just made him feel worse.

Dwight almost forgot how happy and connected and free he used to feel. Sometimes he thought that was just a fantasy – a trick his memory was playing on him. It was hard to believe that a bear that so fat and stupid could have been so happy.

Then he thought, "Of course, as soon as I fix these defects, I'll be a happy, free bear again."

The other animals noticed that Dwight was never at the river playing any more, and began to be concerned for him. So they sent someone to look for him.

Luckily, the animal they sent was Bertie, the bird. Bertie was a very wise bird. She listened to him, and said, "Why don't you tell me what is wrong?"

Dwight was so tired of how he was feeling, and how he was talking to himself, and so tired of feeling like he needed to be fixed, that he told her everything.

Bertie picked up the mirror and brought it over to Dwight. She said, "Look in this mirror and just look at the eyes that are looking at you. Whose eyes are those?"

"They're mine."

"And who are you?"

He thought she was being silly, but he said, "I'm Dwight."

"Keep looking at those eyes, Dwight – see how they are the same bear's eyes, whether you are fat or skinny; whether you are happy or sad."

And Bertie kept whispering things in Dwight's ear so that Dwight would understand that he was the same bear he has always been.

The next thing everyone knew, there was Dwight back at the river, playing and splashing around and laughing. He was the same happy bear they had always known.

Ollie asked him what brought him to his senses.

He said: "I don't have to change anything to be whole. You know how I know? A little Bertie told me so."

You Don't Have to Change Anything

This proposition sounds easy – it sounds like something we already believe. But it becomes one of the hardest to incorporate into our experience.

If this is true, then you can keep your selfishness, your greed, your pain, your disease, or whatever other qualities or problems that stand in your way, and still be whole, and experience life as full, wonderful, and be joyful. That does not sound like how most of us experience ourselves.

"As soon as I lose thirty pounds," "when I don't have as much pain," "when I can sleep more restfully," "if I can quit focusing on my material possessions," "when I start acting out of love, not fear… These are all ways we express a conditional acceptance of ourselves – ways we say, "I have to change to be whole."

Yet the point of unconditional love is to love wholly, without conditions. Experiencing acceptance is a necessary way of experiencing love. Acceptance means accepting all of the person, including his/her qualities or problems you don't like. (Note: this is different from accepting the problem).

Unconditional Love and Acceptance

Learning to offer this kind of recognition of wholeness is not always easy. We do, however, have some models for it. First of all, look at how we feel about pets. A pet is often the object of unconditional love. We see their problems and things we don't like, and we don't withdraw our love. The dog that insists on going to the bathroom where he is not invited is not thrown away or rejected. We may punish him if we believe that's a way of training for different behavior, but we continue to accept the animal, saying, "he's just being a dog."

We also model unconditional love with babies. The baby does a lot of disgusting things, yet we don't reject her – we deal with the poopy diaper, and know that she's just a baby.

Or consider the toddler that is learning to walk. He may walk four or five steps one time; then the next time, go a couple of steps and fall down. We don't say, "You stupid boy; it's unforgivable to fall down; that's not what you're supposed to do; I don't think you'll ever learn; boy, are you dumb!"

It never occurs to us to consider him unacceptable just because he hasn't achieved mastery of the combination of balancing and holding himself upright.

Contrast these examples with how we treat ourselves. Most often, we don't separate the qualities or problems from our self identification.

We don't give ourselves the space of saying, "That greedy action came out of my insecurities; that's how I acted, but it's not who I am; I'm just being a human." Or, "This pain is horrible and I hate it; the 'I' that is underneath and separate from the pain is still a beautiful being."

The qualities and problems which, in a pet or child, we might forgive, or seek learnings from, we use as evidence against ourselves to prove that we're not lovable, not beautiful, not worthy – in short not acceptable.

But we don't have to change to be whole. This step is critical to the transformation we seek. We experience our power, our beauty, and our strength when are able to understand and accept all of ourselves. From that place of wholeness we can choose to make whatever changes we want. It is from that place of understanding and accepting our wholeness that we actually have the power to change our fear, our greed, our pain.

The corollary is, as long as I stand in the position of being so unacceptable because I'm greedy, I'm an incomplete spiritual being who can't participate in changing that part of me that acts out of greed.. Since I'm responsible for my own healing, I have just set up an impossible situation. I have to change to be acceptable, and I have to be acceptable to change. I'm stuck.

The way out is to align with the intention to live out of your wholeness. To bring about that alignment, you clear the emotional level of the energy realm by adopting this truth – "you don't have to change to be whole."

Making the "Heart Decisions"

Rachel's sister is married to a Native American and they live on a reservation in the Southwest. Rachel went to spend a week there. The first day there she found and bought a very special ring. She tells this story of what happened:

"The second day, my sister and her husband took me to a sacred place on the reservation. There I had an experience of energy like I've never had! I could feel energy connecting me to the earth and connecting to my heart in such concrete ways. I sat on a flat rock

130

there, and had an understanding that this was a very spiritual place for me.

Two other times in the week, I had them take me back to that place and sat on that flat rock. Each time I experienced a profound spiritual connection, and would just sit there for an hour and a half or so.

"The day before I was to leave, I once again went there alone. As I sat on the rock, I wondered whether I should leave my ring there as a gift. I was aware of the Native American tradition of leaving a gift for the spirits, and wondered whether I ought to do that. I just wanted to make the "heart" decision; but, couldn't decide what that decision was.

"As I pondered, I took off the ring and imagined myself walking away without it, to see how that felt. Then I put the ring back on and imagined walking away with it, to see how that felt.

"Then something happened like I've never experienced. I became aware that there was a circle of beings at that place. I actually could "see" them and feel them there. They were very old, wise, benevolent Native American spirits. They were kind and concerned with me. They were also very curious to see what I was going to decide about the ring.

"There was no vestment or suggestion from them as to what would 'please' them. They were fine if I left the ring; they were fine if I took the ring; but mostly they were very curious.

"That was the most freeing experience I've ever had!!! I understood that whatever I decided, whatever the 'heart' choice was, was completely acceptable and right.

"Then the heart decision was obvious – I took off the ring, buried it behind the rock, and left it as a connection and gift from me to that place and those beings. I left completely satisfied."

Rachel's story illustrates how we naturally will make "heart decisions" when we are free from the distortions that keep us from our wholeness. When we see that we are whole, we don't have to be concerned that judgments about changing ourselves are necessary. We don't need the moral blackmail of thinking we'll be less if we don't have negative consequences to suffer.

As you reflect on how you are, look at your attitude or state of mind. Often when we evaluate ourselves, we are overly critical and judgmental.

How to be "Whole" and "Human" at the Same Time

If you are to accept yourself as whole, whether or not you change, you must then look at your actions, behaviors and qualities with an attitude of grace and forgiveness. You forgive yourself not for being wrong, but for being human – you don't hold yourself to some standards that you can't meet, then condemn yourself for not meeting them. You look at yourself with love and humor. You intend to do your best – sometimes you succeed and sometimes you don't. When you succeed you celebrate, and when you don't succeed, you forgive yourself, start with a clean slate, and trust that your inherent connection to the light will lead you in the right direction.

Famous athletes like Michael Jordan know how to do this. Throughout a long career, Jordan "failed" to make a basket many times, but kept intending to do his best – and succeeded at having a brilliant basketball career despite the times he didn't "succeed" at making a basket.

As you move to the Energy Tool here, bring those same qualities to this exercise: it is really important to complete this chapter and exercise with an emotional and energetic experience that *you don't need to change to be whole.* Don't be discouraged if it is slow in coming. There is no time limit on getting through all these steps, and you will achieve the experience of your wholeness as you are supposed to.

Wholeness Includes More Than You Know

Finally, it is also important to put into perspective who you are and how much your wholeness includes that you never think of. We tend to notice those things that aren't working, and not notice our miraculous accomplishments. Here are some physical, mental, and emotional examples.

Physical: consider your foot, for example, as a design challenge. This foot holds all your weight, takes you everywhere you want to go; somehow the combinations of bones, nerves, muscles, ligaments, and blood supply have been put together so it is soft, yet strong; accomplishes all the mentioned tasks, is sensitive to heat or pressure to tell you not to step in a particular direction, and works with the rest of your body to move you in a coordinated way.

Just imagine the thousands of actions you do every day without consciously being aware of them: your hands, the nervous system, the circulatory system, the adrenal system, and on and on. Yet often we only notice when they don't work, or we misunderstand how they work: for example, your finger sends pain when you get too close to fire, or your stomach hurts when you eat too much.

Emotional: consider how alive you know you are as a result of your emotions. You tend to appreciate the joyful ones, and not have so much gratitude for the "negative" ones: sadness, fear, depression, anger. Yet, the sad emotions express aliveness and range; the fear tells you what to stay away from (that it can be misleading or based on inaccurate knowledge base doesn't change its positive function); the anger can be energizing, can alert you to new feelings about a situation, and can help you find power and resolve.

Mental: It is unlikely that you give yourself credit for all the many mental accomplishments that you do routinely. When you want to go outside, your brain solves how to move your body, open the door, unlatch the screen, and move to a safe place outside; it then checks to make sure that the ground is level enough to stand on, that you are not stepping into traffic, that the temperature is safe – or suggests steps to take (wearing a coat, for example) that will make it safe.

You can find hundreds of the same kinds of things going on each day. If you don't credit them with being signs of intelligence, try imagining how many steps it would take to program a computer to do the same things, stay aware of the same number of side possibilities, and respond to as many unusual or unexpected circumstances with the same degree of intelligence as you routinely do.

So, as you consider your wholeness, don't forget to include all the parts of your wholeness that are so routine that you don't notice them.

Energy Tool: Opening the Fifth Window

This is a self-healing method for you to clear the emotional aspect of your energy realm for experiencing your wholeness:

1. Get a set of crayons and also retrieve the drawing and papers from the first window, as well as the papers you wrote in response to the second window.

2. Find a quiet place; and, if you like put on some reflective music – preferably something without lyrics.

3. Spend a few minutes just paying attention to your breathing, quieting your mind, and letting yourself relax and focus on listening to the nothingness of the most-quiet place in your mind.

4. For this exercise, assume as true that there is a bigger/wiser you that sits beyond the physical, and that you are looking at the person sitting here from that perspective. From that perspective, keep an attitude of forgiveness and grace for the person sitting here.

5. First take a little time to look at the drawing of wholeness that you created in the first

exercise. Then review the list you made at that time of what wholeness was reflected in the drawing.

6. Next take the writings from the second assignment, and review the blocks identified.

7. Your assignment now is to take crayons, and for each of the blocks in the second assignment, find a way to add a faithful representation of that block to the picture of your wholeness (from the first assignment). If you had an "A" list of blocks (that had neither an "x" or a check mark), you can use that list for this assignment. If that sheet of paper was blank, use the blocks from the first list. *With each addition, add it in such a way that it does not destroy the beauty of the picture.*

8. When you have completed the additions, set the drawing down, and shut your eyes; clear your mind and focus on your breathing, the music (if any) or other sounds in the area, and the feeling of your physical body as you sit there. Do this for several minutes.

9. Now open your eyes and look at the picture of your wholeness as it has been amended in this exercise. Can you experience the beauty of it? Is it as beautiful as before you added the blocks? How is it different? [***If the picture has been "ruined", or the

beauty diminished by the additions, then do the following assignment:

    a. Go to the assignment for step 1, and repeat steps one through 5.

    b. Repeat steps one through eight of this exercise. This time, however, add to your assignment to *find a way to add the blocks and keep the beauty of the overall picture.*

10. You now have a picture of your wholeness that includes the blocks you identified as a part of it. Congratulate yourself on being open enough and wise enough to incorporate this perception into your energy body, as well as your consciousness. Once again sit and simply feel your physical body. Close with whatever reflections you have about the exercise – and with an expression of appreciation to the total being that is you for having the willingness to do this process.

Thank you for your participation.

CHAPTER 12

THE SIXTH WINDOW: AWARENESS OF YOUR WHOLENESS WILL CHANGE YOU

You don't "have to" change to be whole. However, once you assume awareness of your wholeness, you will change: you'll experience yourself differently in your life, and be able to choose to make changes more easily.

The Story: Wendy Wildflower

Just on the edge of the woods lies a meadow surrounded by a lot of trees. The sun beams into the meadow like a friendly big brother, bathing the meadow with warmth, light, and a sense of gentle well being.

On one side of the meadow, you can see a big patch of tired looking gray-green plants, leaning away from the sun.

138

Our heroine is one of those plants: Wendy Wildflower. Wendy Wildflower and her friends, who are also all wildflowers, are confused. She and her friends all wake up when it's night, and stay asleep when the sun comes up. They have been told since they were just little seedlings that the sun is very dangerous, and that you can't think right when the sun is beaming on you. So plants must train themselves to go to sleep in the morning when the sun is coming up, and then wake up during the nighttime when the sun isn't there.

And that's just what Wendy and her friends do. But there is a problem with that. They all know they are flowers, but they never seem to bloom. They wake up and talk all night, and go to sleep in the morning. They have "learned" that they stay a gray-green, unhealthy-looking color; and that "blooming" like flowers supposedly do, is apparently just a myth.

But Wendy senses there is something more. Part of her is missing; she yearns for something. She is also curious about what happens during the day when the sun is out.

So one morning, Wendy just pretends to go to sleep until all the other plants have snuggled in for the day. She watches the sun come into the meadow.

It feels so good!

It feels so right!

She gets very excited!! Why, this opens and warms and invites a whole part of her that she hasn't been getting to feel. As the day progresses, she gets another new feeling – an opening – and low and behold! She blooms. There is a pretty blue flower that comes out at her top. How exciting!

She can't wait to show the other plants.

When the other flowers begin to wake up, Wendy says, "Look!"

But guess what? As night fell, her bloom closed up, and she looks just like she did last night.

So the other flowers are not impressed. Wendy tells them about how great it is to stay awake in the day – but they think she's crazy.

"You're not being responsible, dear." says one of the older flowers, whom they all call "Mum." And of course because she's so tired, she soon falls asleep – so they have further proof that she is not really accepting reality.

Wendy wakes up the next morning and spends the day awake, with her pretty bloom – and the next, and the next.

Soon there is a much healthier-looking green glow to Wendy's stem. One night three of her best friends – Iris, Rose, and "Daffy" (well, her whole name is "Daffodil" but that's SO old fashioned) decide to trust Wendy. The next day they stay out in the sun with her.

One has a purple bloom; one rose; and the other yellow. They are so excited – and you can see what happened from there.

When they all reported the same experience, the rest of the flowers tried it.

And within a week the flowers were waking in the daytime and sleeping at night. And they all felt warmer, prettier, and happier. They all became aware of that part of them that likes the sun.

When you walk across the meadow now – over on that side – you don't see this patch of gray-green stems; instead, you see a patch of beautiful and colorful flowers, waving excitedly and happily in the breeze.

Moral: When you live in awareness of your wholeness, it changes you.

How You Are Changed

Remember our little boy playing with the blue car? If he is aware that he is just playing a game, remembers that the other boy is somebody he really likes to play with, and he enjoys the sunshine and out-of-doors, he has a different experience than if he thinks *everything* depends on the blue car winning.

Similarly, as we move into wholeness, our larger perspective helps make the day-to-day matters less ultimate, and lets us experience the blocks and distortions as just that – blocks and distortions – not diminishments of ourselves. We can then more easily stay connected with our natural curious, present selves, and life is a more joyful and peaceful experience.

We can also choose to experience blocks and distortions differently. You know you don't have to change the nature of yourself to change a block. (I'll fix *me* by losing thirty pounds). Now you keep the same basic "whole" self, and shift one expression of that (I choose to have thirty less pounds). Without feeling that the issue determines your value, it is easier to look dispassionately, see what lessons or value the "block" may have, and choose to keep it or not.

In this window, we are now bringing the mental level of the energy realm into a cleared place for changing the underlying intention. This is both the last preliminary step, and the place to integrate all the rest. Here we integrate the energy realm, bring the physical and emotional into alignment with the mental, and we integrate the energy realm with the material realm in the same way. Our integration of belief systems, emotions and physical bodies can now receive and hold the changed intention in a way that is internally consistent throughout the entire energy field.

Two Steps Forward, One Step Back

Do not be fooled by what appears to be "backsliding." We often accomplish changes of energy patterns, and feel really good about ourselves; then act or experience the old pattern one day. When this happens, we doubt the validity of our transformation. We are caught in a "stair-step" image: we think, "I learn this much, now I'm here; I learn something else, now I'm one step higher on the ladder." Then when we find we've acted out something that was three rungs lower, we become discouraged.

Energy moves in vibrations – waves. The process of energetic change is a series of overlapping waves of expansion, contraction, expansion, etc. Envision energetic advancement as a series of loops where we move forward to a new realization or understanding, then loop backward to a behavior; loop forward farther than before, and then loop back, but not as far back as before. We are never as "good" as we think at the front of the loop, and never "bad" as we think at the back of the loop.

Instead of reproaching yourself with discouragement ("I haven't done that since I was a sophomore in high school; I must not have learned anything!"), understand the process, and approach your "old" behavior with curiosity ("I must be at the back of the loop; I wonder what I'll learn or experience as I go to the front of the loop this time!"). Knowing and recognizing the process of energetic change and its vibrations is a part of being aware of your wholeness.

More Choice About Blocks

The integration of this part of wholeness with your mental functioning at the energy realm carries another freeing aspect. Moving out from under the shadow of the distorted perspective that your blocks need to be "fixed" yields a better ability to change your energy and behavioral patterns. In other words, there are more things you can change voluntarily. The flip side of this additional ability is that you may also be more hesitant to remove blocks and distortions, because you now understand why you might have created them and what purposes they may serve in your over-all energy system.

If you do not understand why you have a headache, you would not want to remove it, without understanding its significance. If the headache is a result of a growing brain tumor, for example, you wouldn't want to "cure" the headache without also understanding that the headache is a sign of a more serious problem that needs to be addressed.

You might decide "I want to be thirty pounds thinner." You might even perceive the extra weight as a distortion – it keeps you from feeling good, it causes knee problems, you don't like how you look, etc. Before you integrate the awareness of your wholeness, you see this weight as a distortion of you, and that when the weight is gone you can be better.

Now look at it from the perspective of wholeness: you are a beautiful being, whether or not you have the thirty pounds. From this perspective, the extra weight still stresses your knees, and probably isn't how you choose to structure your physical body as you go through the rest of your life. You don't have this distortion (the thirty pounds) by accident, however. Before you decide that it's time to choose differently, you will want to understand the energy message of the thirty pounds and make sure that it is not vital to some other aspect that you are ignoring. This energy message is carried in the energy field. As an example, you might discover an accompanying belief system ("bigness" equals "power") that led you to build yourself with this extra weight.

Simply having taken a larger perspective and living from wholeness may have resolved this issue. You now experience your power; thus, the reason for the extra weight is no longer there. You can now choose to let go of the weight and find that the physical manifesting of that is now relatively simple. In other words, when you are choosing to eat differently and exercise differently from reasons that don't have underlying contradictions, you can accomplish the task without angst. You'll choose to change your weight with the same neutral emotional charge as you choose to change a green shirt to a blue one on a given day.

In the example, you were clear about what the energy of the extra weight attached to. Other issues may not be so clear. And even when you sit and examine particular blocks or diseases from the aspect of wholeness, you may not understand them. Sometimes consultation with another person – or an energy healer – will help to uncover the deeper aspects that are not apparent.

Remember that we are still working in the energy realm, talking about what you can accomplish by changing the energy. Resources for helping change at the material realm can unlock the resistance to changing the whole being.

In the example involving weight, the energy might involve some underlying belief system and emotional matters that you carry in the material realm. Working with your energy (either by yourself or with an energy healer), and consulting with a cognitive therapist (psychologist, counselor, etc.), might help you clear the underlying difficulty on the material realm.

Similarly, if you have difficulties on the physical realm, you can supplement energy work by consulting someone who works on the physical, material body (M.D., chiropractor, etc.).

Synchronicity

There is a wonderful synchronicity in the universe that operates in support of your healing. When you make the changes in the energy realm, you will discover that other aspects of your life on the material realm open up with new opportunities. You may not be aware of the effect of an energy change on the mental level; however, at that same time, a new book or a new idea or a new friend's concept comes along that truly speaks to your material belief system in such a way that your understanding shifts.

There will be new stimuli, new friends, new physical remedies, new ideas, and on and on. You may have started experiencing this already. The manifesting of new opportunities on the material realm in all aspects (physical, mental, and emotional) is a part of the universe's energetic response to your changes. In other words, you create a different energy field that attracts a different response from the universe.

Remember, even as you assume these new and exciting choices, there will be moments, or days, when you feel like the "old you." But you can keep the perspective so that those moments don't seem so devastating and don't last so long. You can balance your pain with your curiosity about where it might lead you.

Energy Tool: Opening the Sixth Window

This is a self-healing method for you to integrate the mental aspect of your energy realm and all other aspects for experiencing your wholeness:

1. Get a set of crayons. Also retrieve the final drawing you did in the fifth window.

2. Find a quiet place; and, if you like, put on some reflective music – preferably something without lyrics.

3. Spend a few minutes just paying attention to your breathing, quieting your mind, and letting yourself relax and focus on listening

to the nothingness of the most-quiet place in your mind. For this exercise, assume as true that there is a bigger/wiser you that sits beyond the physical, and that you are looking at the person sitting here from that perspective. From that perspective, keep an attitude of forgiveness and grace for the person sitting here.

4. Now place the drawing of your wholeness, as you completed it in window 5, in front of you and reflect on it.

5. As you reflect on the drawing, see if you can find one piece – one detail – one part of a color and shape that you might improve by changing. In other words, you are being invited to amend one of the parts you added, and change the expression of it in your drawing by changing it. You don't need to remain faithful to a true expression of the block, just change the drawing in the way that you are aesthetically drawn to do so. Your goal is to add beauty to the drawing by changing one aspect of it. Now take the crayon(s) and change that part of the drawing.

6. When you are through, again place the drawing in front of you: appreciate the beauty of the whole being reflected in the drawing.

7. See if you can remember which block you expressed in the part of the drawing that you

changed; if you can, identify the purpose or reason for the block as it was originally in your field. Does the change you made eliminate the block? Or does it change it in some way? Does the purpose for the block still exist in your energy field? Are you ready to eliminate or choose a different energy expression of the issue identified with the block?

8. Notice that you have the power to change the entire drawing; that you can make changes in one or more aspects without disturbing the beauty of the whole; that you didn't need to make something ugly in order to have an excuse to change it – that you are free to increase the beauty of the drawing (and thus the being) without having to make any of it ugly.

9. Once again sit and simply feel your physical body. Close with whatever reflections you have about the exercise – and with an expression of appreciation to the total being that is you for having the willingness to do this process.

Thank you for your participation.

CHAPTER 13

THE SEVENTH WINDOW: BEING AWARE OF YOUR WHOLENESS IS MORE FUN THAN LIVING IN IGNORANCE OF IT

You have arrived at the culmination of the process. Here we move to the actual changing of your intention for how you experience yourself in the world.

The Story: Merry Meadow

This is the story of the day the meadow learned its name.

Moody Meadow was just at the edge of the woods, a little way from the village. She was a nice field of green grass, with some flowers over on one side, and a circle of trees around it. She was a pleasant enough looking meadow, with a nice meeting place in the middle and a little stream running across one side. But Moody Meadow was bored and depressed.

"Nothing ever happens here," she thought. "Oh sure, sometimes animals, and even some people stop by; and the plants keep going on about what plants go on about; but it is just – well – sameness."

Moody Meadow sighed and frowned, continuing her unhappy litany.

'The forest has all those trees that can be used for building things; and the village has lots of people that accomplish things; and even the farm fields make themselves useful for growing food. But I'm just sitting here."

One day, about noon time, as Moody was sitting there, being grouchy, and only "kind of" paying attention to what was going on, a little girl named Dawn, who had this wonderful sparkly light, came into the meadow and sat down. As soon as she did, Buddy the Bird, who was celebrating having just built the best nest in the West, flew in and perched on a tree at the edge of the meadow; Dwight the bear waddled out of the woods and headed toward Dawn's friendly light.

Wendy Wildflower and her flower friends started waving in the breeze, when who should drive up but Terri the '56 Thunderbird, resplendent in her new bright wax job that emphasized her beautiful red color. She was bringing Don, a very wealthy man from town – and he had pulled out a red and white checked table cloth, which he put on the ground, with gifts for everyone: a basket with sandwiches for him and Dawn, honey for Dwight, birdseed for Buddy, a lavender-mist spray to refresh Wendy Wildflower and her friends, and a pair of big rubber dice that could hang from the rear-view mirror for Terri.

Everybody got very excited about the gifts and the chance to be together; and Moody Meadow suddenly realized that it was a beehive of joyful activity. There was the colorful splash of the pretty wildflowers – yellows, browns, blues, violets, pinks, etc. – all the colors of the rainbow on one side: and the bright red beauty of Terri the Thunderbird on the other. Buddy the Bird was singing a beautiful song (and several of his friends joined in). Terri the Thunder"bird" (a bird of another sort) discovered that she could honk her horn in a rhythm that joined in the singing. Dwight the Bear was using the background of the music to do what he does best – the comic routines that made the other beings laugh and feel good.

Dawn and Don were sitting on the blanket, enjoying the sounds, the sights, and the good food and good times; Dawn's sparkly light was at its effervescent best – lighting the whole meadow with sparkles in the sunlight.

Moody Meadow realized that this was what the meadow was – alive to all its parts. She was so much more than she had been aware of. It felt so much better. And she decided in that moment that from now on, she no longer would be "Moody" Meadow. Now her name is Merry Meadow.

And so she has stayed to this very day.

> *Moral: It's more fun to live in awareness of the wholeness than it is to be in ignorance of it.*

The New Intention

"Fun" is perhaps too limited a word for the difference you will be experiencing. True, life is more "fun," but that is just a part of it. When you understand yourself from a place of wholeness, you like your life better, you experience your connection more, your purpose more, and you live from a place of inner peace and, yes, "joyfulness."

How do you live out of this new intention? The first surprise is that this will not be hard. Whenever you align more closely with your intention, it gets easier. This is because you are not fighting against a deeper part of yourself in choosing what you do and how to be. In fact, if life is a struggle, that is an indication that you are out of synch, misaligned, with your deeper intention.

The line of intention is like a river running deeply within you. You live your life in the flow of that river. When you get at cross purposes with the river, it is like trying to hang on: as you hold on, the river is actually pulling against you, and you have to work at being where you are. When you align yourself with that intention, you release the hold, allowing yourself to move in the rhythm of the river. Everything is going downstream with you at the same pace, there is no struggle, and it is actually easier.

As you are created, your deepest intent is to be aware of and live out an understanding and appreciation of yourself as a whole being. So this change doesn't make it harder, it makes it infinitely easier – for you are dropping into a place you've already intended to be.

The New Perception of the Old Intention

When I talk about "changing your intention," I am really making a misstatement. You are changing a "perception," of your intention, not the "intention" itself. The intention is already there. The river has always been there; you just haven't been aware of it. You are now gaining that awareness.

Why did you ever block that perception of your intention? You created the blocks and distortions to help accomplish the purpose of your life. The creative process of living our lives is to throw ourselves out into an illusion of separation, and then find our way back. Thus, from a place of unity, we have come into a material realm that is in duality; then we find our way back to the unity. One piece of that process is to move to a larger perception of yourself, which is what you have done (or reinforced from having already done) in the process of assimilating this book. As you live out of the place of wholeness now, the purpose in creating those blocks will become clearer.

How do you know that now is the right time to clear these distortions and move into this new awareness? One of the lessons that comes with this bigger perception is how huge "synchronicity" is. We've heard there are no accidents; that coincidences are really a combination of events that the universe/we use to bring about results that wouldn't "usually" be expected; that there is a right time for matters to happen, and that what is needed for them to happen is there at that time. This isn't what we came to expect from the perception of reality adopted from the major culture we were born into.

However, you have already moved beyond that perception. You have paid attention to experiences in your life that really can't be explained as coincidences; they accomplish too much and work out too well. It is actually necessary to close our minds to many of life's experiences to try to pretend that they are just "accidents."

This combination of events is not one of those accidents. Now is the time that this material has come your attention. Now is the time that you have done the exercises. Now is the time for you to start living out of your wholeness. Whether or not your mind totally understands, in your heart you have committed to this time as the time to "jump into this river."

Intention, Not "Will"

"If 'intention' is this easy," you say, "why didn't I get rid of _____ (fill in the blank – my block, my pain, my weight, etc.) a long time ago? I really have wanted to get rid of it."

It is necessary to distinguish between "intention" and "will." The statement of will is, "I want." The statement of intention is "I connect."

When we want to make things happen, or want to make changes, the tool we have is "will." Our willpower helps us accomplish things, helps us stay with tasks even when they are difficult, and helps us carry out our goals. Will operates, however, from the personality.

Intention, on the other hand, operates from a connection to a higher, or larger perspective of purpose.

In the illustration of the red car/blue car, the boy with the blue car has an *intention* to stay outside, play, and enjoy the company of our friend. His *will* is to do all those things, but also to get the blue car to win.

When our will is aligned with intention, it is a great tool. When our will is at cross purposes with our intention our life is harder; and we may even help defeat (momentarily, at least) the purposes of intention. Again in the illustration: the will to stay outside is aligned; the will to get the blue car to win starts getting frustrated.

The little boy got so involved in "wanting" the blue car to win that he got upset, and started projecting anger on his friend with the red car. From the larger perspective there is really no intention about the red car or blue car winning. But the will's investment makes the intention to "enjoy the company of the friend," harder or impossible to experience at that moment.

In our lives, we often see things that we want, and try to bring them about by our will. Intention is connecting with that underlying river. When will is wanting to impose matters that aren't aligned with intention, trying to force our will actually impedes our ability to live from intention.

Aligning with a perception of yourself as whole and keeping that in your consciousness is an act of intention. As such, it will be easy and without resistance. When one tries to eat a healthy diet as a matter of will, it is a struggle and very difficult. When one is aligned with the intention of having a healthy body, choosing healthy foods becomes natural and is easier to accomplish, even though the desire for the unhealthy foods will still remain. The desire will just have much less power.

Surrender and Patience

Another word for this process of aligning with intention is "surrender." Surrender is the key because it emphasizes for you what you are surrendering to. That river of intention is the guide. You may describe and experience it as "spirit,' as "the Holy Spirit," as your bigger/wiser self's best guidance for you, or in any of a number of other ways. It matters only that you yield to that, let your "will" get out of the way, and go as directed. Aligning with intention is that simple.

What is the tool that will allow you now to change the intention? In a word, your tool is patience. The ease of intention comes from a perspective of you as a whole being, allowing the flow of your creative energy; the resistance to changing intention comes from the personality's desire to keep you safe by blocking that flow. You will remember we talked about this in Chapter Eight.

In order to activate the intention, you need to notice your resistance. Overcoming that resistance by force (which is our first tendency) demands total involvement of the will. Trusting that you are bigger than the resistance will activate the intention. If you allow yourself to be, undergo whatever resistance you experience, but – with patience and tolerance – keep looking from the larger perspective, ultimately the resistance cannot prevail. You are aligning with a greater truth, the truth of who you are, so that reality will ultimately emerge. You simply need to connect with the intention, and have patience.

Patience may seem like a tall order – it's probably not been one of the strongest qualities you have offered yourself. But once again, synchronicity will come to your aid. From the larger perception of your bigger/wiser self (the mother at the window), you can see how much the resistances you throw up to transformation are really attachment to red car/blue car issues. Let yourself have those, and let go of those, without being condemning or judgmental. Just remember that patience will allow your resistance to melt away faster than any amount of impatient yelling or cursing at yourself.

Energy Tool: Opening the Seventh Window

This is the process of connecting at your deepest intention level with your wholeness.

1. Get some blank paper, pen to write with: find a quiet place; and, if you like put on some reflective music – preferably something without lyrics.

2. Spend a few minutes just paying attention to your breathing, quieting your mind, and letting yourself relax and focus on listening to the nothingness of the most-quiet place in your mind.

3. Take the blank piece of paper, and carefully write on it the following: "I live experiencing the wholeness, and staying consciously aware of that wholeness."

4. Set that piece of paper in front of you, so that when your eyes are open, you can see it without moving.

5. Now take some time to review what your wholeness is: start with your physical body – pay attention to each part of your physical body; then move to your emotional body – pay attention to and list in your mind all the different emotions and feelings you can remember having in the last several days; then move to your mental body – pay attention to how much information you process, how many things you figure out on the elementary level (how to open a door, for example), how many beliefs you hold, how many separate items of information are held in your mental body.

Now move on to your energy realm: just pay attention for a moment to the energy that you hold and carry in you; then pay attention to the intentions you have, how many different things you intend; pay attention to the framework you have created for holding all the emotions and belief systems, and how there is in you something that holds all those together in a pattern.

Finally, in reviewing your wholeness, look at the bigger/wiser you – the one that stands beyond this personality and advises, watches, and observes what your personality does; this is the place from which you can observe the overall framework and all your actions, feelings and thoughts.

6. Now close your eyes and allow yourself to experience all of those ideas and feelings

you have just reviewed by just being in the space and fullness of this incredibly huge and filled person that you are.

7. Open your eyes and look at the paper: Read it aloud.

8. Let that sentence permeate your consciousness, take it into your self as if you were physically taking the energy of the sentence into your energy body: imagine it moving from the paper into your outer energy field, into your physical body, into your inner energy field, and settling in the very middle of your energy field, at the very middle of your heart.

9. Speak it aloud again, this time as if it were coming from the center of your heart, up through your throat and out into the world: "I live experiencing the wholeness, and staying consciously aware of that wholeness."

10. Now shut your eyes and experience yourself with this intention fully a part of your being, from deeply within you out to the edges of your consciousness. Feel the presence of this wholeness and your awareness of it as little particles of energy and consciousness that are infused into all parts of you.

11. When you have completed the process, once again sit and simply feel your entire self. Close with whatever reflections you have and with an expression of appreciation to

the total being that is you for having the willingness to do this process.

Thank you for your participation.

————————————————

Now that you have opened the seven windows to wholeness, I recommend that you write this phrase on a piece of paper: *I live experiencing the wholeness, and staying consciously aware of that wholeness*. Post it where you will see it several times a day. You might put it on your refrigerator, your bathroom mirror, or any similar place. Or you might make that statement your "screen saver" on your computer. The point is, of course, to let your consciousness at all levels have an ongoing reminder that can reinforce your alignment with the intention.

CHAPTER 14

GUIDANCE FOR LEADING A GROUP TO EXPERIENCE THE SEVEN WINDOWS

For some people, the accomplishment of the exercises and experience of the seven steps is best done in a group. Group energy helps people take the time to focus on each of the exercises and supports each individual in the process. You can also share and discuss results and reflections on each of the tools. This chapter gives suggestions as to how that has best worked for people.

Leading a Group to Experience the Energy Tools

A. Preliminary to each meeting:

1. Each of the tools can best be experienced if one of the members of the group acts as the facilitator. The leadership can be

passed around among the members of the group, and the leader for each time should be chosen ahead of the meeting.

2. The leader for each step should review the step beforehand, and assemble the necessary materials.

3. Prior to the meeting, the leader does the energy tool him/herself. (Have your finished product available, but don't share it with the group until everyone has done the exercise.) You are now free to lead the exercise without the distraction of trying to do your own process at the same time.

4. At the beginning of each group gathering, going around the circle with a short "check-in" from each member will bring the group to a common focus.

5. The leader should decide whether it is appropriate in each setting to start with a discussion of that night's window, or whether just to read the directions set forth in the Energy Tool and move directly into doing the steps of the Energy Tool.

B. First Meeting: First Window: You are Already Whole:

6. Start the meeting with a check-in; then move directly into the Energy Tool exercise, saving discussion for the end.

7. Pass out the materials (crayons, blank paper, and pens), and put on some soft, meditative-type music. Suggest to the group that they maintain silence throughout the actual exercise.

8. Lead the group by reading aloud paragraphs 2 through 5 of the Energy Tool: then allow some time for the drawing.

9. As people are nearing completion of the drawing, read paragraph 6.

10. When all have finished their drawing, tell them to put the picture of their energy body in front of them and just look at it and reflect on it.

11. Read paragraph 8 verbatim: then give them time to make the list.

12. When all have completed, invite each to share their drawing and list, and let the discussion flow from that sharing. Additional questions to keep the discussion going might be: "What surprised you about your drawing?" "What surprised you about your list?" "Are there other obvious items that you would have expected to be on the list?"

"How do you feel about your drawing and/or your list?"

13. Collect the drawings and papers and keep them for use in future meetings.

14. Close the evening with a reminder as to time and place of the next meeting and choice of leadership. Ask the group to pay attention to their lives over the next week, noticing where these elements of wholeness they have identified are present in their lives.

C. Second Meeting: The Second Window: *Your Wholeness is Covered Over by Belief System Disorders:*

   a. Again, the leader will have done the exercise before the meeting; start the meeting with a check-in.
   b. Pass out pens and paper; put on meditative music.
   c. Read paragraphs 2 and 3 from Step 2 energy tool; allow time for completion.
   d. Read paragraph 4; allow time.
   e. Read paragraph 5; allow time.
   f. Read paragraph 6, and once again allow time for completion.
   g. Lead the group through meditative and actual physical experience by reading paragraphs 8 through 10, allowing time for the actions indicated.

h. After the meditative time, bring the group together for reflections and sharing – including their experience and feelings about both the lists they made, and the exercise.

i. Collect the papers and keep them for future meetings.

j. Close the evening with a reminder as to time and place of the next meeting, choice of leadership, and whatever closing you like.

D. Third Meeting: The Third Window: *You Already Know How to Clear the Distortions.*

a. The leader will have done the exercise before the meeting; start with a short check-in.

b. Put on meditative music, if desired.

c. Lead the participants through the meditation and exercise by reading paragraphs 2 through 10 of the energy tool, step 3. Allow time as you do so for them to do each of the indicated activities.

d. Ask them to sit quietly a few minutes and just honor themselves in that place

e. After the meditative time, bring the group together for reflections and sharing. Have them describe what occurred, and share their feelings as this unfolded.

f.   Close the evening with a reminder as to time and place of the next meeting, choice of leadership, and whatever closing you like. You may suggest that they repeat the exercise of touching and expanding their core essence into their hands and through their bodies as a daily meditation.

E. Fourth Meeting: The Fourth Window: *Aligning with the Intention to Recognize Your Wholeness is the First Step.*

a.   The leader will have done the exercise before the meeting; start with a short check-in.

b.   Put on meditative music, if desired.

c.   Lead through meditation by reading aloud paragraphs 2 through 8 of the energy tool, step 4, allowing them time for the reflections at the appropriate places.

d.   Read paragraph 9, and lead them through the statement,
   "If it's in my best and highest interest, I align with the intention to hold the core essence vibration in my body and my energy field, and to hold the awareness of it in my consciousness."

e.   Read paragraph 10, and lead them through the statement again.

f.   Invite them to continue to sit in silence in reflection.

g.   After the meditative time, bring the group together for reflections and sharing. Let them share and explore aligning with wholeness might mean in their lives, how that feels, and any other reflections on the evening.

h. Close the evening with a reminder as to the time and place of next meeting, choice of leadership, and whatever closing you like. They might be sent forth with the invitation to continue to notice when they experience being aware of their wholeness, when they don't, and what causes them to forget. It is good at this time to remind people that they are just at the fourth step of a seven step process, so they need not be discouraged if they are not doing it "perfectly" yet.

F. Fifth Meeting: The Fifth Window: *You Don't Have to Change to Be Whole*

a. The leader will have done the exercise before the meeting; start with a short check-in.

b. Pass out a set of crayons to each member, and also the drawings they created from step one, and the lists and papers they made in steps one and two.

c. Put on meditative music, if desired.

d. Read aloud paragraph 3 of energy tool, step 5.

e. Tell the group: "It is important to notice those aspects of wholeness that we don't always think of. Here are physical, emotional and mental examples:"

f. Read the paragraphs starting with "Physical," "Emotional," and "Mental," concluding with the sentence ending, "... parts of your wholeness that are so routine that you don't notice them."

g. After a moment for them to absorb the above, read paragraphs 4, 5, and 6 from the evening's Energy Tool, and allow time to follow the instructions.

h. Read paragraph 7; allow time.

i. Read paragraph 8; allow time.

j. State to the group: "Now open your eyes and look at the picture of your wholeness as it has been amended in this exercise. Can you experience the beauty of it? Is it as beautiful as before you added the blocks? How is it different?" Allow time for reflection.

k. Tell the group: "You now have a picture of your wholeness that includes the blocks you identified as a part of it. Congratulate yourself on being open enough and wise enough to incorporate this perception into your energy body, as well as your consciousness." Allow reflection, and bring the group back to the present.

l. After the meditative time, bring the group together for reflections and sharing. Share the pictures, what was added, and how they feel about the beauty of the picture now. See what, if anything, that indicates to people in their lives.

m. Close the evening with a reminder as to the time and place of next meeting, choice of leadership, and whatever closing you like.

G. Sixth Meeting: *The Sixth Window: When You Live in Awareness of Wholeness, It Changes You.*

a. The leader will have done the exercise before the meeting; start with a short check-in.

b. Pass out a set of crayons to each member, and also pass out the drawing he/she did from step 5.

c. Put on meditative music, and remind the group, as always, to maintain silence through the meditation and exercise.

d. Read paragraphs 3, 4, and 5, from Energy Tool, Step 6, and allow time.

e. Read paragraphs 6 and 7; allow time.

f. Conclude the meditation portion by reading paragraph 8, with a short time of silence afterwards.

g. After the meditative time, bring the group together for reflections and sharing. Share the pictures, what was added, and how they feel about the beauty of the picture now. See what, if anything, that indicates to people in their lives.

h. Close the evening with a reminder as to the time and place of next meeting, choice of leadership, and whatever closing you like.

H. Seventh Meeting: *The Seventh Window: It's More Fun to Live in Awareness of Wholeness than to Live in Ignorance of It.*

a. The leader will have done the exercise before the meeting; start with a short check-in.

b. Pass out paper and pens; put on meditative music if desired.
Have each person write on their paper, in big, easy-to-read letters: "I live experiencing the wholeness, and staying consciously aware of that wholeness."

c. Have people focus on their breathing, get quiet, and relax. Read paragraphs 4, 5, 6 and 7 from Energy Tool, Step 7. Allow time, and lead in reciting the statement.

d. Read paragraphs 8 and 9 and allow time for the speaking.

e. Read paragraph 10.

f. After the meditative time, bring the group together for reflections and sharing. Note that this is the last meeting, and invite reflections on the process.

g. Close with whatever closing you like. You can suggest to people that they post the statement, "I live experiencing the wholeness and staying consciously aware of that wholeness" on their refrigerator, bathroom mirror, as their screen saver, or anywhere else that it can serve as a reminder in their day-to-day affairs.

FINAL NOTE TO THE READER

Thank you for pursuing this adventure with me. I hope that the process has helped you to reclaim something more of yourself and that you have found it profitable and useful. For me, as I reached that place from which I could say, "I live experiencing the wholeness and staying consciously aware of that wholeness," I experienced surrender. I was able to be a curious, awestruck, excited participant in the day-to-day unfolding of my own life.

At the beginning of this book, I recounted my experience as a teenager of standing at the edge of the universe, and being afraid to jump off.

Forty years later, when I surrendered to the Wholeness Intention, I finally found myself having jumped into that place. To my delight, instead of falling into a place of terror, I was embraced, supported, and inspired.

I wish for you a similar experience.

I would love to hear from you about your experience with this book. For this or any questions or comments, please contact me through my website: *www.CoreStarEnergyHealing.com*, where there is a button for sending me e-mail.

About the Author

Jim Crabtree is the Founder of Core Star, Inc., Director of the Core Star Healing Training Program, and originator of the process for opening the seven windows to wholeness. In conducting more than 7,000 individual healing sessions and teaching workshops, seminars, and classes on the Human Energy Field for over fifteen years, Jim has provided both clients and students with a wealth of experience and information on self healing and well being. Graduates of the Core Star three year Healing Training Program carry these techniques and knowledge to their clients across the United States.

Now Jim has incorporated the unique human energy field techniques for connecting with wholeness into a self-help book, *The Seven Windows of Wholeness*.

Jim graduated from the four-year Barbara Brennan School of Healing and taught classes there for two years. Prior to his work with energy, Jim was a lawyer with a successful trial practice. In addition to his formal training at the Barbara Brennan School of Healing, Jim has practiced and studied Therapeutic Touch, Reiki, and other energy modalities with teachers and healers throughout the United States, Europe and South America. Readers may learn more about him and his work, and correspond with him on his website at www. CoreStarEnergyHealing.com.

Printed in the United States
126165LV00001B/30/A